SHORTCUT 4
518 CONFIDENCE QUOTES

by LINKED IN AND TOWN HALL ACHIEVER OF THE YEAR
EY NOMINEE ENTREPRENEUR OF THE YEAR
GRAND HOMAGE LYS DIVERSITY
WORLD TOP100 DOCTORS

Dr BAK NGUYEN, DMD

TO EASE THE WAY TO YOUR PERSONAL LEGEND, ONCE YOU ARE OUT OF YOUR QUEST OF IDENTITY.

by Dr BAK NGUYEN

ISBN:: 978-1-989536-77-3

Published by: Dr. BAK PUBLISHING COMPANY
Dr.BAK 0096

DISCLAIMER

ABOUT THE AUTHOR

From Canada, **Dr. BAK NGUYEN**, Nominee Ernst and Young Entrepreneur of the year, Grand Homage Lys DIVERSITY, LinkedIn & TownHall Achiever of the year and TOP 100 Doctors 2021. Dr Bak is a cosmetic dentist, CEO and founder of Mdex & Co. His company is revolutionizing the dental field. Speaker and motivator, he wrote 72 books over 36 months accumulating many world records (to be officialized). His books are covering:

- **ENTREPRENEURSHIP**
- **LEADERSHIP**
- **QUEST OF IDENTITY**
- **DENTISTRY AND MEDICINE**
- **PARENTING**
- **CHILDREN'S BOOKS**
- **PHILOSOPHY**

In 2003, he founded Mdex, a dental company upon which in 2018, he launched the most ambitious private endeavour to reform the dental industry, Canada wide. Philosopher, he has close to his heart the quest of happiness of the people surrounding him, patients and colleagues alike. In 2020, he launched an International collaborative initiative named **THE ALPHAS** to share knowledge and for Entrepreneurs and Doctors to thrive through the Greatest Pandemic and Economic depression of our time.

In 2016, he co-found with Tranie Vo, Emotive World Incorporated, a tech research company to use technology to empower happiness and sharing. U.A.X. the ultimate audio experience is the landmark project on which the team is advancing, utilizing the technics of the movie industry and the advancement in ARTIFICIAL INTELLIGENCE to save the book industry and to upgrade the continuing education space.

These projects have allowed Dr Nguyen to attract interests from the international and diplomatic community and he is now the centre of a global discussion in the wellbeing and the future of the health profession. It is in that matter that he shares his thoughts and encourages the health community to share their own stories.

"It's not worth it go through it alone! Together, we stand, alone, we fall."

Motivational speaker and serial entrepreneur, philosopher and author, from his own words, Dr Nguyen describes himself as a dentist by circumstances, an entrepreneur by nature and a communicator by passion.

He also holds recognitions from the Canadian Parliament and the Canadian Senate.

SHORTCUT 4

518 CONFIDENCE QUOTES

by Dr BAK NGUYEN

INTRODUCTION
BY Dr BAK NGUYEN

INTRODUCTION

by Dr. BAK NGUYEN

This time I am a little ahead, a few hours after the completion of **SHORTCUT volume 3 - LEADERSHIP**, the first tome of **RISING**. I am saying that I am ahead because neither Apple Books nor Amazon has made it available yet. Is that a compliment?

Well, yes, since Apple Books and Amazon usually distribute my books with hours (less than 24 hours) after its submission. It has been like this since the last year, after that, I have set the world record of writing 72 books within 36 months, 2 books a month on average! This year, I am aiming for 100 within 4 years, that's 4 more books, on top of the world record!

Oh, and by the way, Barnes and Noble are now publishing my books within 36 hours! This is a new mark for me! Apple Books, Amazon and now, Barnes and Noble have been my biggest fans! Thank you for the vote of confidence.

Even if I am bold and like to jump in head first, I had my share of doubt entering this challenge. Lately, the **Alphashow**, with a chance to reach Netflix and/or Amazon Prime is taking much of my time, and that's time that I can't create from thin air. Interviewing, editing, and broadcasting take time on a linear basis, the process cannot be done in parallel, it is one step after the next. That took much of last Spring.

So I fell behind writing books. Now entering the last month of writing before the celebration of 4 years as an author, I still have, including this one, 5 **SHORTCUT** volumes to write and 2 more books to replace **COVIDCONOMICS** and **CRYOTOCONOMY** that won't be ready in time. So that's 7 books in 31 days.

That's 4.43 days per book! Last year, to finish my world record challenge, I had to write a book every 8 days for 8 straight weeks. This time, it is even worst! Am I confident? I must say that I am encouraged by the numbers.

A week ago, as I was still on vacation, travelling and working on **COVIDCONOMICS**, my math was telling me that I had a little more than 4 days per book with 9 to write, 4.11 days to be exact. With 2 books written and published within a week (**SHORTCUT** volume 2 and 3), my numbers are improving to 4.43 days per book.

0.33 days per book, is that significant? Well, watching the Olympics Summer Games, Tokyo 2020, I must say that I am pretty happy with the result. The difference between

Gold and no podium is often less than a second in the pool and on the tracking field.

More than the Gold and the podium, there is the stream of records. I was reading this morning about Penny Oleksiak who just win her 3rd Olympic medal in the game, elevating herself at as highest decorated Canadian Olympian of all time with 7 medals, that gave me a boost in inspiration and in motivation.

It is about set the record straight and clean before each event. Then, as you are giving your best in that event, you stand up, take your win or loss and move on to the next one, uncompromised. And yes, numbers matter, in the pool, on the field, in the books.

So yes, writing a book, I am all in while writing that book. Even at a record pace, as soon as I am done with that book, I have to shake it off to be available for the next one, and the one after that. Even if I am a sprinter, I am running a marathon of sprints.

To compensate for the fatigue of the races piling up, I saw a reflection watching another great athlete, Caeleb Dressel, the American superstar swimmer, who, at the time of this writing, won 5 Gold medals at the Tokyo 2020 Olympics.

Looking at Caeleb, I noticed a serenity before each of his races. After his first Gold medal, he seems even calmer, sure of himself. Just like Penny Oleksiak, he has to shake off his last victory to be available for the next race, but from his last victory, you can feel that he is keeping something from his last win, his **Confidence**!

And that is what this journey is about, Confidence. Yes while healing and growing, you needed and found Confidence.

"The real Confidence that will take you to another level, the Olympian's level, is the Confidence that you are building moving through your wins, ladder by ladder."
Dr. Bak Nguyen

That's quote #2445. Just like Penny and Caeleb, I am moving forward with ease, knowing that I have in me to do it, not just better, that I can still push for more and that is done without burning all of my fuses all at once. You too, now that you have started your rise, will experience that feeling of supreme calm, insurance, and humility!

And yes, humility is a key emotion of this trade to not break your **synergy with the Universe**. Because that is what fuelled our Confidence, the synchronization of our vibe with a universal pillar of the Universe. We are energy much more than we are matter. Never forget that.

And forget those who are telling you that life is not a race. Life is a race. You can either run ahead, follow in the peloton or fall behind, playing catching-up. Stop the denials and embrace life as it is, dynamic. That said, we are not all running the same race, and that's the key to our Unity. But we each have our races to run and to finish.

So here it is, the 4th volume of the **SHORTCUT** series, **CONFIDENCE**. This journey, just like the last one, will be comprised of 4 parts: Confidence, Evolution, Empowerment, and the famous 77. May you find inspiration, motivation, and, above all, your Confidence.

This is **Shortcut volume 4, CONFIDENCE**. Welcome to the Alphas.

Dr. BAK NGUYEN

PART 1
"CONFIDENCE"
by Dr. BAK NGUYEN

Confidence, this should be one of the easiest chapters that I have to write in carrier. Not just because that I was born confident but because growing up, I let Conformity take it away, leaving me with simply a **WANNABE** shell, the state where you know that you are something and where you do not feel it inside.

That void grows slowly to allow **Doubt** to appear. Once doubt is there, it simply eats up your mind. So even my **WANNABE** status was now part of the past, as I stop believing and knowing. All of my attributes were now based on the medals and licences that I was granted by Society.

Then, as I found true love, my heart started to beat with an echo, the **Echo of Confidence**. As I felt true love, beating in my chest, Confidence reappeared. Now it was the mind that did not want to give in. I was broken, but inside out. I felt Confidence within my heart and body, but I was in denial. That left me very vulnerable, as I started winning thanks to Confidence, but the driver in place (my mind) simply ignored that strength to keep doubting.

That's the irony of my story, as people saw a confident leader in me, I was doubting myself. Above everything, I did not want to resume to my **WANNABE** state. So I kept growing and servicing people, and my Confidence grew from the results of my actions.

I still grew, but I was nowhere near the calm of **Caeleb Dressel,** the Olympian multiple Gold medalist, moving ahead with the Confidence built from each of his last wins. He is moving up and building, multiplying. Me, because that I was doubting, I was still winning but adding up horizontally my wins and Confidence. It was much less efficient and much more time-consuming.

Then, I moved forward while trying to keep those I love around me. I gave them everything that I got, showing them what I have learnt and newly mastered.

I was so into helping them that, as my lower body was aiming forward, all of my upper body was turning back to lend a hand to pull those I loved. I was torn inside and could not hold that position for too long, and I did anyway.

Then, I even left my advancement to walk back, standing behind those I love to empowered them to move forward. What I called empowerment, they called pressure. And then, the unthinkable happened. They even jumpep on my back to sabotage me, trying to keep me intentionally behind.

I was lucky enough that the sabotages did not touch my core. I healed from true and pure love, the love of my best friend and wife and from the love of my young son.

Then, I met with a higher spirit who told me that I have to forgive myself. With his words, something snapped in me. That took years, but he left the cloud of doubts in my mind and I was finally whole, feeling my Confidence beating and pumping in my chest and veins. I was free to test its power. My wings grew back and I rose.

I am rising as a **force of nature** and a **kind tornado** ever since. I am rising and flying smoothly and calm, and my strengths are unmatched where I bet on my talents and set my mind to. I grew into a kind tornado because I was reunified, I had Confidence both in my heart and in my mind. And this is the underline story that you will be reading moving forward within this journey of **CONFIDENCE**.

Confidence, not just the kind that we are born with but also the story of how one could have lost it and learn to recapture it much later in life as ones is handicapped with **doubts**, **average**, and **jealousy**.

"Confidence is sexy."
Dr. Bak Nguyen

We each have our unique story. We each have our demons and doubts. Some were born with Confidence and somehow are stuck in **WANNABE** mode. I can help you. Some other did not have Confidence in their early days but had to earn each of their stripes moving forward. I can help you too.

And to those champions born with Confidence who challenged a force of nature bigger than themselves and got crushed with failures, I can help you as well.

This is a journey of empowerment, of healing, one rising up with Confidence beating in our chest. As we gathered what we have received from birth, the **WILLPOWER** and the **DIVINE**, that's **CONFIDENCE** flowing in our veins.

As we are moving ahead and left doubt to settle in because we stayed polite, because we wanted so much to fit in or because it was forced down our throat, we will have to make peace with the past, regrets, and denials to heal. And then, we will have to grow back from the ground up.

As you remembered your old days as a champion and now cast aside because of one fatal failure, one injury that pinned you down ever since, you too can heal and come back to, not your former glory, but an even greater one.

The **River of Life** is flowing forward and there is no force to reverse that. Being Confident and in sync with the Universe, you are swimming in its flow and even maybe driving the current forward. This is when you feel invincible, in **the zone** as the athletes are calling it.

To those in business, we are referring to that state as **MOMENTUM**. Well, I know a way to reach momentum. I also know the way to fix the broken, putting back the pieces in the minds and those in the heart, I know because I've been there.

If this was an easy chapter to write, it was a painful and long journey to walk but now that I am through, that I made peace with the past, everything is so clear and it made so much sense.

All of that, I knew for a while by now. By looking at the calm of **Caeleb Dressel** and his wins in the water, the imagery became crystal clear. Caeleb is not done yet, his tornado is just starting. I was writing and kept pushing to know where is the limit, as long as I remain calm and in sync with the Universe, I too, am not done yet!

This journey is one to find your inner force, your Confidence, and to empower you to walk your Destiny, your legend!

This is **Shortcut volume 4, CONFIDENCE**. Welcome to the Alphas.

Dr. BAK NGUYEN

PART 2

"95 CONFIDENCE QUOTES"

by Dr. BAK NGUYEN

0396
FROM SYMPHONY OF SKILLS
"Arrogance is not the bragging of our knowledge but rather the denial of our ignorance."

Dr. Bak Nguyen

0397
FROM LEADERSHIP, PANDORA'S BOX
"Leave, live, and lead!"

Dr. Bak Nguyen

0398
FROM IDENTITY, ANTHOLOGY OF QUESTS
"Bear the name, be the one, taste the fame!"

Dr. Bak Nguyen

0399
FROM IDENTITY, ANTHOLOGY OF QUESTS
"The songs we wrote shall be for others to sing. We, we should sing the songs of others."

Dr. Bak Nguyen

0400
FROM IDENTITY, ANTHOLOGY OF QUESTS
"A hero is the embodiment of hope because he, himself will never give up the hope to find his unity."

Dr. Bak Nguyen

0401
FROM IDENTITY, ANTHOLOGY OF QUESTS
"We were all born free, free to choose,
free to accept."
Dr. Bak Nguyen

0402
FROM IDENTITY, ANTHOLOGY OF QUESTS
"Trust your emotions and your body since
they will always tell the truth!"
Dr. Bak Nguyen

0403
FROM IDENTITY, ANTHOLOGY OF QUESTS
"A man united with his heart will always knows
the way to or the way back. The head doubts,
the heart knows!"
Dr. Bak Nguyen

0404
FROM IDENTITY, ANTHOLOGY OF QUESTS
"Listen to your body, that's your only truth
that will never lie"
Dr. Bak Nguyen

0405

FROM IDENTITY, ANTHOLOGY OF QUESTS

"Conquer, don't steal, seduce, don't lie,
charm and be kind."

Dr. Bak Nguyen

0406

FROM IDENTITY, ANTHOLOGY OF QUESTS

"Call me a star and I will shine.
Call me a rock and I will hold.
Call me dad and I will care.
That's how I matter to you.
To me, I was I."

Dr. Bak Nguyen

0407

FROM INDUSTRIES' DISRUPTORS

"I don't care. are we going?
I'll worry about the details later."

Dr. Bak Nguyen

0408

FROM INDUSTRIES' DISRUPTORS

"Silences and waits are over."

Dr. Bak Nguyen

0409
FROM INDUSTRIES' DISRUPTORS

"It was more crazy than sexy."

Dr. Bak Nguyen

0410
FROM THE POWER BEHIND THE ALPHA

"I must have been either crazy or just very confident."

Dr. Bak Nguyen

0411
FROM THE POWER BEHIND THE ALPHA

" I am the mascot! I am just surprised that
in my couple, we chose the least attractive one
to be showcased to the world! "

Dr. Bak Nguyen

0412
FROM THE POWER BEHIND THE ALPHA

" I am a man of my word, of my many words. "

Dr. Bak Nguyen

0413
FROM THE POWER BEHIND THE ALPHA

"Only confident people really know how to bow."

Dr. Bak Nguyen

0414
FROM MOMENTUM TRANSFER
" Momentum: stronger than the why,
the feeling and the cause is the who! "
Dr. Bak Nguyen

0415
FROM MOMENTUM TRANSFER
" Do the most with what's in hand.
There will never be a perfect setup."
Dr. Bak Nguyen

0416
FROM MOMENTUM TRANSFER
" The difference between a philosophy and a doctrine
is that the doctrine has an enforcer to dictate fear
while the philosopher was betting on
the strength of his thoughts alone."
Dr. Bak Nguyen

0417
FROM HYBRID
"Attraction is hunger, curiosity, and Love."
Dr. Bak Nguyen

0418

FROM HYBRID

"Will we trust in ourselves enough to build on what
we feel rather than on what we know?"

Dr. Bak Nguyen

0419

FROM HYBRID

"Confidence with the kiss of Doubt
will slowly turn into Pride."

Dr. Bak Nguyen

0420

FROM LEVERAGE COMMUNICATION INTO SUCCESS

" The new joke around me is how many times
can I change the world!"

Dr. Bak Nguyen

0421

FROM LEVERAGE COMMUNICATION INTO SUCCESS

"Confidence is sexy and people like sexy!
That is also why and when jealousy will show
its ugly head!"

Dr. Bak Nguyen

0422

FROM FORCES OF NATURE

"The result was confidence, strong
and pure self-confidence."

Dr. Bak Nguyen

0423

FROM FORCES OF NATURE

"Few will heal completely from the infection of
expectation. For the rest of their lives,
they might be chasing ghosts."

Dr. Bak Nguyen

0424

FROM FORCES OF NATURE

"Humility is to accept what we are
and to stop pretending."

Dr. Bak Nguyen

0425

FROM THE BOOK OF LEGENDS, VOLUME 1

"At least as a rockstar,
I can let my emotions flow freely."

Dr. Bak Nguyen

0426
FROM SELFMADE
"Never burden yourself with medals."
Dr. Bak Nguyen

0427
FROM THE RISE OF THE UNICORN
"I am used to move forward, a single win at a time."
Dr. Bak Nguyen

0428
FROM THE RISE OF THE UNICORN
"No experience is a mistake if you learn from it.
And then, leverage that."
Dr. Bak Nguyen

0429
FROM THE RISE OF THE UNICORN
"The only way I know how to play is all in."
Dr. Bak Nguyen

0430
FROM CHAMPION MINDSET
"No confidence can grow from a doubting heart."
Dr. Bak Nguyen

0431
FROM CHAMPION MINDSET
"What you feel is best will also be
what you will do best."
Dr. Bak Nguyen

0432
FROM CHAMPION MINDSET
"If you do what you feel,
you know that it also feels right."
Dr. Bak Nguyen

0433
FROM HOW TO WRITE A BOOK IN 30 DAYS
"The tunnel vision of a hero is great
in emotional experiences, but poor in wisdom."
Dr. Bak Nguyen

0434
FROM HOW TO WRITE A BOOK IN 30 DAYS
"Be bold, be honest."
Dr. Bak Nguyen

0435

FROM HOW TO WRITE A BOOK IN 30 DAYS

"Even bold, I don't like to pretend to something that I am not. I might project, but not pretend."

Dr. Bak Nguyen

0436

FROM POWER, EMOTIONAL INTELLIGENCE

"The first rule of influence, be confident!"

Dr. Bak Nguyen

0437

FROM POWER, EMOTIONAL INTELLIGENCE

"Listen, accept, respect, and grow.
Those are the keys to Confidence."

Dr. Bak Nguyen

0438

FROM POWER, EMOTIONAL INTELLIGENCE

"Confidence is to be whole and to be in HARMONY."

Dr. Bak Nguyen

0439

FROM POWER, EMOTIONAL INTELLIGENCE

"Confidence is a journey."

Dr. Bak Nguyen

0440

FROM POWER, EMOTIONAL INTELLIGENCE

"The fewer the words, the better."

Dr. Bak Nguyen

0441

FROM BRANDING

"I am open because I am confident and strong enough to embrace what's coming. If I needed protection, that's because I wasn't strong enough."

Dr. Bak Nguyen

0442

FROM BRANDING

"I faced my problems, but emotionally, I looked for a way to avoid them."

Dr. Bak Nguyen

0443

FROM HORIZON VOLUME ONE

"I am no survivor. I am a driver, and I will thrive."

Dr. Bak Nguyen

0444

FROM HORIZON VOLUME TWO

"I am a westerner, and I am a unifier.
Call me a banana if you must."

Dr. Bak Nguyen

0445

FROM HORIZON VOLUME TWO

Because intolerance is just that: the insecurity of one.

Dr. Bak Nguyen

0446

FROM HORIZON VOLUME TWO

"I am bold, walk my talk and do not take
myself seriously. That's the recipe!"

Dr. Bak Nguyen

0447

FROM HOW TO NOT FAIL AS A DENTIST

"No one is immune to doubts. But one can learn
to keep his doubts under control."

Dr. Bak Nguyen

0448

FROM HOW TO NOT FAIL AS A DENTIST

"I am prideless and confident.
That's a dangerous mix of efficiency."

Dr. Bak Nguyen

0449

"Flexibility does not mean to be spineless, it means to be confident enough to listen and to please."

Dr. Bak Nguyen

0450

"Confidence does not mean to be full of yourself and to have all the right answers. Confident means to be secured enough to be open to listen and to discover new alternatives."

Dr. Bak Nguyen

0451

"The day that I stopped trying to be James Bond and accept my fate as Shrek, that day, my charisma and presence grew exponentially. "

Dr. Bak Nguyen

0452

"To have a place, be useful. To earn your place, start walking the journey that your heart leads you on."

Dr. Bak Nguyen

0453
FROM MINDSET ARMORY
"As open-minded as I am,
I never fully leave my ground."

Dr. Bak Nguyen

0454
FROM MINDSET ARMORY
"The heart has always been and will always
be stronger than the mind, since it was from nature,
the divine."

Dr. Bak Nguyen

0455
FROM HUMILITY FOR SUCCESS
"Power is looking for submission.
Confidence is looking to help."

Dr. Bak Nguyen

0456
FROM HUMILITY FOR SUCCESS
"Authenticity is the best shield against doubt."

Dr. Bak Nguyen

0457

FROM PLAYBOOK INTRODUCTION VOLUME 2

"I am so confident now that I can explore all the avenues, not feeling threatened, and allowing me to remove most of my blinded sides."

Dr. Bak Nguyen

0458

FROM PLAYBOOK INTRODUCTION VOLUME 2

"Play ALL-IN and never give up. This is attractive!"

Dr. Bak Nguyen

0459

FROM AMONGST THE ALPHAS, VOLUME 1

"Don't look for approval, look to overwhelm. And then, do not care and keep doing it."

Dr. Bak Nguyen

0460

FROM AMONGST THE ALPHAS, VOLUME 1

"Power isn't something you hold too tight close to your chest since it might kill you."

Dr. Bak Nguyen

0461
FROM AMONGST THE ALPHAS, VOLUME 1

"Now, what is authority? Who is looking to impose?
Basically those with insecurity."

Dr. Bak Nguyen

0462
FROM AMONGST THE ALPHAS, VOLUME 1

"This game is the game of evolution, you can win
if you do not evolve. Well, motivation is a pretty
strong leverage."

Dr. Bak Nguyen

0463
FROM AMONGST THE ALPHAS, VOLUME 1

"Free from FEAR, that's the first wealth you will find,
depth and nuances."

Dr. Bak Nguyen

0464
FROM AMONGST THE ALPHAS, VOLUME 1

"To fight, to win, to achieve
are three very different things."

Dr. Bak Nguyen

0465
FROM AMONGST THE ALPHAS, VOLUME 1
"The price to being different will eventually be your best deal if you keep pushing."
Dr. Bak Nguyen

0466
FROM AMONGST THE ALPHAS, VOLUME 2
"Be generous, grateful, and genuine, not naive."
Dr. Bak Nguyen

0467
FROM RISING
"To gain influence, one needs to be confident first. And to be confident, one needs to drop his/her insecurities."
Dr. Bak Nguyen

0468
FROM RISING
"Confidence is your only way to conciliate your need for security with your desire to rise."
Dr. Bak Nguyen

0469
"Openness can absolutely not coexist with insecurity."
Dr. Bak Nguyen

0470
FROM EMPOWERMENT
"Addressing insecurity is to feed.
To feed it, is to empower it."
Dr. Bak Nguyen

0471
FROM EMPOWERMENT
"Exclusivity is about insecurity.
Loyalty is about character."
Dr. Bak Nguyen

0472
FROM THE MODERN WOMAN
"Insecurity leads to fear, fear leads to intolerance.
Intolerance will ask for control and
control is power-hungry."
Dr. Bak Nguyen

0473

FROM TOUCHSTONE, LEVERAGING TODAY'S PSYCHOLOGICAL SMOG

"Confidence is to make a call and be comfortable to face its outcome. Arrogance is to think that there is no other way."

Dr. Bak Nguyen

0474

FROM TOUCHSTONE, LEVERAGING TODAY'S PSYCHOLOGICAL SMOG

"Doubting will not help nor solve anything. Being flexible and aware will."

Dr. Bak Nguyen

0475

FROM TOUCHSTONE, LEVERAGING TODAY'S PSYCHOLOGICAL SMOG

"Take doubt away and the odds of success are now in your favour."

Dr. Bak Nguyen

0476

FROM TOUCHSTONE, LEVERAGING TODAY'S PSYCHOLOGICAL SMOG

"There is a fine line between confidence and pride. It's about who or what is in control."

Dr. Bak Nguyen

0477
FROM TOUCHSTONE, LEVERAGING TODAY'S PSYCHOLOGICAL SMOG
"When confidence and openness are,
past, present, and future, start to blend
into one single vibe: possibility."
Dr. Bak Nguyen

0478
FROM ALPHA LADDERS VOLUME 2
"Confidence is to know our nature and function.
Humility is to know that there is so much more."
Dr. Bak Nguyen

0479
FROM MIRRORS
"If anything, confidence is humility, the power to
embrace the truth and to be whole."
Dr. Bak Nguyen

0480
FROM MIRRORS
"Control is neither good or bad. It is a mean
to keep doubt at bay until one's confidence is strong
enough to fill the void."
Dr. Bak Nguyen

0481
FROM MIRRORS
"In the heart, I found a solution,
the key to a great cheat!"
Dr. Bak Nguyen

0482
FROM MIRRORS
"Confidence is humility and
gratitude embodied in one heart."
Dr. Bak Nguyen

0483
FROM MIRRORS
"We are energy, we are alive. staying still, we will rot."
Dr. Bak Nguyen

0484
FROM MIRRORS
"Confidence is key to a steady and smooth evolution."
Dr. Bak Nguyen

0485
FROM MIRRORS
"Awareness is calm, light, eternal."
Dr. Bak Nguyen

0486

"Just let go and be. the best way to be in control is to give up control."

Dr. Bak Nguyen

0487

"I know what I am.
I am looking for pleasure and worth."

Dr. Bak Nguyen

0488

FROM THE CONFESSION OF AN OVERACHIEVER

"If you never talk about yourself, it is then all about your doubts and fears... even when you were not concerned!"

Dr. Bak Nguyen

0489

FROM THE CONFESSION OF AN OVERACHIEVER

"Women look for confidence."

Dr. Bak Nguyen

FROM TO OVERACHIEVE EVERYTHING BEING LAZY

"With confidence, you are silencing doubts
and keeping fear at the gate."

Dr. Bak Nguyen

This is **Shortcut volume 4, CONFIDENCE**. Welcome to the Alphas.

Dr. BAK NGUYEN

PART 3

"EVOLUTION"

by Dr. BAK NGUYEN

Evolution is much more than **Growth**, it is growing while finishing to heal. It is Growing, compiling the victories, and about all, it is finding your true power within your **Confidence**, not the one you've received from birth but the one that you are building on your own, one adventure after the next.

You know me well by now. I am not someone who will eternalize on definitions, which to me is mainly an opinion.

"Definitions are opinions, forced down the throat opinions. Even with great intentions, never forget the true nature of a definition."
Dr. Bak Nguyen

That's quote #2446. Never forget that statement, it is for your own sake. You can build upon a definition for a while, just to get used to the environment and the laws around, but keep an open mind that everything is relative and that everything is in constant evolution, changing through time and space.

And that's the main difference between **Growth** and **Evolution**, the relative part. Growing, you are getting bigger, stronger, better, compared to your old self, your old environment, your old system of reference. Growing also gave you the means to look at a higher horizon and to keep going.

Once through the **glass ceiling**, you realized that you can move in 3D, from horizon to horizon, keep moving up but there is also a multitude of horizons sideways that can be explored too. In each of these horizons, you can zoom in and zoom out. Now the possibilities are really infinite. What you learnt growing from your first horizon was not the laws, the people, or the events, but the skills to move up, down and now, sideways.

From one level to the next, the laws changed, the event fades and the people dimmed down very quickly until you zoom back in. That's relativity. If you were wondering if there is a way to mute drama, here's your answer:

"To mute drama, rise to the level above.
To resume dram, zoom back in."
Dr. Bak Nguyen

That's the 2447th quote. You see, growing meant to learn to swim, to breathe, and to stir. Now at the evolution stage, it is about where are we going and learning from each experience, each journey.

I will never stretch this one enough but the biggest trap of growing is to lose your **flexibility** of mind and heart and to fall into the temptation to set everything in stone. That might work for a while but only as you are zooming down. You know that it is a lie and, just like pride, you will be spending the rest of your vital energy span to feed that lie until you run out of life.

Someone else might take over and so on and so on. Many of our beliefs systems are built that way. That's ok if that was your choice, but if you were born inside of one of these systems, as you awake, you will be seeing the system for what it is, a management system to keep control in the name of protection. Then, you can choose to help its maintenance, to walk away, or to knock it down.

I will advise you to think twice before knocking down any system. Please be aware of the consequences and especially, the collaterals damages that you will be causing. No system is perfect. That said, the system is still nurturing a certain stability and security to those inside of that system. Don't knock it down without a better alternative, or alternatives.

And once you will think of the alternatives, you will realize how complex and time-consuming it is to build a new system. I am too lazy for that. Me too, I was tempted to knock down an imperfect system as I see one but the idea of building a new one from the ground up showed me a fact: I quickly realize that I was not as smart nor nearly as committed to make it my life commitment.

So very quickly, I resumed to another alternative instead, patching up the system and empowering internal small changes and improvements instead.

If the system was flawed at its base, why waste any more time to patch it will you ask? Because it is a kinder solution to those you are still inside of the system, to these people, it is their home and they will fight and even give their lives for its defence, even if the home that they are defending is a prison cell.

I am not stating this out of insensibility, trust me, it still pains my heart to fact this words. It took me much time, healing, and wisdom to let go of the past, the anger, and the blame to become calm and powerful.

And only once calm, I understood that no one likes to be forced. What I've been through is not easy and very painful. Not everyone is ready to go to such lengths. To not inflict on others the kind of pain that I suffered myself, I learnt to respect the timing and wish of everyone.

As a doctor, the first rule before engaging is to get consent. Well, at least, on that, my training stuck with me. I am looking for consent first before interfering. And even as I received consent, I am very aware of the collaterals and the ripple effects of each of my actions. Nothing is ever perfect, that's my reminder, that's what will keep me balance. I am acting to patch the system and to empower one to start his or her journey, nothing more.

As I came to rise, I am doing so with the respect of the forces surrounding me, not starting a war at each turn. At the end of the day, my ledger will be comprised of all the good I did minus all the collaterals that my actions and their ripple effects they caused. That is keeping in mind that I, myself, have done nothing wrong!

This is a great example of what Evolution is. It is to grow while keeping the balance and harmony intact.

"Evolution is to change while keeping the surroundings and the balance intact. It is both a wisdom and an impossible task."
Dr. Bak Nguyen

That's the 2448th quote. That's not a definition but a statement. If you can replace it with a better one, please let me know, I will be pleased to improve my reality. As said, at the beginning of this chapter, evolution is to grow knowing that everything is changing and that nothing will last or stay the same.

Growing was bipolar, you go up or down. Evolving, you discover the universe and surf possibilities. Ever wonder how some people are always positive and somehow, manage to live in **abundance**? Sure, some are lucky. But to the majority of them, it is because they have discovered more than one horizon, more than a set of rules, and more than one way to find happiness.

Younger, I was taught that if I wanted a better future for myself, I needed to work hard. So I did. Then, every time that I work hard enough to get to the next level, I face a new challenge that will require me to work even harder.

Eventually, I stopped asking the question, and I looked at the challenges as opportunities.

Today, I can do within a day what before would have taken me a year to accomplish. Do I work as hard? I don't know, I stopped asking the question a long time ago. What I know is that I gain much in time efficiency.

What I also learnt travelling the journey of growth and evolution is that the ascension does not always go hand in hand with the **Quest for Happiness**. Earlier on, things were simpler. I was happier each time that I reach a higher level. Passed a certain point in life, these 2 lines diverge drastically. It does for everyone. And this is where you've reached your *glass ceiling*, travelling the pyramid of Maslow:

SELF-ACTUALIZATION

ESTEEM

LOVE/BELONGING

SAFETY

PHYSIOLOGICAL NEEDS

THE PYRAMID OF ABRAHAM MASLOW

You are stuck between **LOVE/BELONGING** and **ESTEEM**. That's the end of your growth and the beginning of your **EVOLUTION**. From this point on, you have to take responsibility for your actions, choices, and growth, not just in the sense of being punished if you cross a line, but in a much broader sense: that the consequences of your actions may be affecting much more people than you alone.

Growing inside of a system, within the confinement of your internal **DAM**, you alone faced the consequences. Now, the safeties are off and you will have to bear the burden of each of your decision.

Don't be like that, rejoice, it is serious but it can be pretty fun too! This is where real life begins! To move ahead, an **open heart** will keep the horizons available. An **open mind** will keep you flexible to navigate even when the laws of physics are changing as you are moving.

Vision will keep you in the right direction (for you). **Compassion** will help your ledger. **Empowerment** will open new doors and lower resistance (friction).

This may not be the only way through the *glass ceiling* but it is one that I know and understand, And the steps are proven. Now it is still for you to walk through your **glass ceiling** and to see for yourself the multitude of horizons possible. Trust me, **abundance** is right there, that's your first reward as you have reached the next level, **EVOLUTION**.

This is **Shortcut volume 4, CONFIDENCE**. Welcome to the Alphas.

Dr. BAK NGUYEN

PART 4
"81 EVOLUTION QUOTES"
by Dr. BAK NGUYEN

1284

FROM LEADERSHIP, PANDORA'S BOX

"The secret of the evolution of mankind lies in the wisdom of working together."

Dr. Bak Nguyen

1285

FROM IDENTITY, ANTHOLOGY OF QUESTS

"We were animals who learned to sing. And then, we became humans."

Dr. Bak Nguyen

1286

FROM IDENTITY, ANTHOLOGY OF QUESTS

"In the past we tried to standardize everything. Today we should stop and decide who we are. So we can customize our future..."

Dr. Bak Nguyen

1287

FROM PROFESSION HEALTH

"After our whole, our kind! Let us stop being apes!"

Dr. Bak Nguyen

1288

FROM AMONGST THE ALPHAS, VOLUME 2

"Fears transmitted are mostly the boundaries of the last generation."

Dr. Bak Nguyen

1289

FROM INDUSTRIES' DISRUPTORS

"It seems that human evolution is finally catching up with the evolution of the cpu."

Dr. Bak Nguyen

1290

FROM INDUSTRIES' DISRUPTORS

"The Internet has empowered the era of entrepreneurs!"

Dr. Bak Nguyen

1291

FROM INDUSTRIES' DISRUPTORS

"If it can be improved, what are we waiting for? Everyone will benefit from it!"

Dr. Bak Nguyen

1292

FROM INDUSTRIES' DISRUPTORS

"Today, keynote speakers are filling
the gap left between our universities and the
evolution of life and technology."

Dr. Bak Nguyen

1293

FROM AMONGST THE ALPHAS, VOLUME 2

"Millennials are evolution and natural selection
proclaiming their progression on
the pyramid of Maslow!"

Dr. Bak Nguyen

1294

FROM AMONGST THE ALPHAS, VOLUME 2

"Were angels a different species created by God or
the relics of an old memory of our own kind?"

Dr. Bak Nguyen

1295

FROM INDUSTRIES' DISRUPTORS

"The new is still unproven, but today, it is sexy!"

Dr. Bak Nguyen

1296

"What were once hidden parts of the story are today the frontline of your story."

Dr. Bak Nguyen

1297

FROM CHANGING THE WORLD FROM A DENTAL CHAIR

" People change, you change, respect that and deal with it."

Dr. Bak Nguyen

1298

FROM THE POWER BEHIND THE ALPHA

" A heart does not evolve, it simply grows and retracts."

Dr. Bak Nguyen

1299

FROM THE POWER BEHIND THE ALPHA

"It was easier to discover novelty than to filter the old."

Dr. Bak Nguyen

1300
"Time and Space change everything.
To stay relevant, we must evolve."
Dr. Bak Nguyen

1301
"Averaging down... that's not evolution,
it's extinction, from an evolution's standpoint."
Dr. Bak Nguyen

1302
"No one really changes, we simply evolve
and gain more nuances."
Dr. Bak Nguyen

1303
"Our body will adapt by reducing the production of
the hormonal respond as technology will compensate
by increases its pace and reach."
Dr. Bak Nguyen

1304
FROM LEVERAGE COMMUNICATION INTO SUCCESS
"The new is neither good or bad.
It can be great if you take the time to master it."
Dr. Bak Nguyen

1305
FROM FORCES OF NATURE
"To keep evolving, comfort zones are oasis to
replenish at, then, the journey continues."
Dr. Bak Nguyen

1306
FROM THE BOOK OF LEGENDS, VOLUME 1
"As immigrants kids, proving yourself is always
somewhere on the table, hardwired into
our core beliefs..."
Dr. Bak Nguyen

1307
FROM SELFMADE
"You can't stand in the way of evolution.
You can help or stand aside, the choice is yours."
Dr. Bak Nguyen

1308
"The main trade that we should transmit is the mean
to adapt, the desire to reshape and the ability
to ask questions. "
Dr. Bak Nguyen

1309
FROM KRYPTO
" To eat was good enough to the animal kingdom.
To be happy is the legacy of human evolution."
Dr. Bak Nguyen

1310
FROM KRYPTO
" Evolution and Legacy are
what should united all of us "
Dr. Bak Nguyen

1311
FROM KRYPTO
" Evolution rather than revolution.
It will required, wisdom and flexibility,
not just determination and courage."
Dr. Bak Nguyen

1312

FROM KRYPTO

" Feel to learn. This time, it wasn't that expensive."

Dr. Bak Nguyen

1313

FROM KRYPTO

"So let's be better than animals and take
the survival part out of the equation once and for all."

Dr. Bak Nguyen

1314

FROM KRYPTO

"The human factor of life is to thrive,
the animal side is to survive."

Dr. Bak Nguyen

1315

FROM POWER, EMOTIONAL INTELLIGENCE

"Like anything else, gathered intelligence
has an expiration date."

Dr. Bak Nguyen

1316

FROM POWER, EMOTIONAL INTELLIGENCE

"Even if the ocean is much closer to us, it was easier to reach out in space than to dive deep in the ocean."

Dr. Bak Nguyen

1317

FROM THE POWER OF YES, VOLUME 1

"We attract what we genuinely are."

Dr. Bak Nguyen

1318

FROM HORIZON VOLUME TWO

"The evolution is within the unknown and the new. If your future is proven, you are mainly rewriting the past, once more."

Dr. Bak Nguyen

1319

FROM HORIZON VOLUME TWO

"The only way to evolve is to adapt."

Dr. Bak Nguyen

1320

FROM MINDSET ARMORY

"Human evolution has come to an age that the one holding the sword is now the target,
not the king anymore."

Dr. Bak Nguyen

1321

FROM HUMILITY FOR SUCCESS

"To be humble is to be aware of our changing place in a bigger and forever changing Universe."

Dr. Bak Nguyen

1322

FROM HUMILITY FOR SUCCESS

"If you want to bet on a sure value, bet on change!"

Dr. Bak Nguyen

1323

FROM THE ENERGY FORMULA

"Our fore and founding fathers were very clever to build values into our Identity."

Dr. Bak Nguyen

1324

FROM THE ENERGY FORMULA

"The layers of civilization started to weight on our primary goal and instincts. It never stopped doubling down its control since."

Dr. Bak Nguyen

1325

FROM THE ENERGY FORMULA

"No one had to teach us how to eat, to seek shelter or to have sex. Those were hardwired."

Dr. Bak Nguyen

1326

FROM SUCCESS IS A CHOICE

"To evolve is much easier than to change. but often, that wasn't a choice. it was just the timing."

Dr. Bak Nguyen

1327

FROM THE 90 DAYS CHALLENGE

"The flaw in the system is the by default."

Dr. Bak Nguyen

1328

FROM THE 90 DAYS CHALLENGE

"Acting by default will kill us all while we are asleep at the wheel."

Dr. Bak Nguyen

1329

"Evolution does not always come
with great feelings. "

Dr. Bak Nguyen

1330

FROM RISING

"No one can stand in front of evolution,
just like no one can resist the power of time.
So, the only smart alternative left is to provoke
and ride evolution and time."

Dr. Bak Nguyen

1331

FROM AFTERMATH

"Changing is never something we welcome easily."

Dr. Bak Nguyen

1332

FROM AFTERMATH

"The paradox of our evolution is to have grown
into a collective of individuals."

Dr. Bak Nguyen

1333

"Better a smaller change that will last
than a in-dept one that will fade."

Dr. Bak Nguyen

1334

FROM AFTERMATH

"Adapting their mastery to the present and
immediate needs is reinventing."

Dr. Bak Nguyen

1335

FROM RELEVANCY

"For the first time within our lifetime,
all interests aligned. The age of competition is over,
the age of collaboration has begun."

Dr. Bak Nguyen

1336

FROM MIDAS TOUCH

"Habit does not go with evolution.
Comfort does not go with evolution."

Dr. Bak Nguyen

1337

FROM TORNADO

"The world is changing, with or without you.
At best, you are adapting forward."

Dr. Bak Nguyen

1338

FROM TORNADO

"Never underestimate the idle instinct of people."

Dr. Bak Nguyen

1339

FROM TORNADO

"Real lasting change is a flow, not an impact."

Dr. Bak Nguyen

1340

FROM TORNADO

"An idea is an impact. A philosophy is a flow.
One will last, one will be swallowed."

Dr. Bak Nguyen

1341

FROM TORNADO

"Change must be inspired, not imposed
to be sustainable."

Dr. Bak Nguyen

1342
FROM BOOTCAMP
"Evolution is not about accumulating
but about experiencing."
Dr. Bak Nguyen

1343
FROM THE UAX STORY
"I understood that a change, to be sustainable
has to be kind and sensitive to its own impact,
good and collateral."
Dr. Bak Nguyen

1344
FROM 1SELF
"It is always time to change, but somehow,
it is never the right timing."
Dr. Bak Nguyen

1345
FROM 1SELF
"Moving up, the air might be scarcer,
but in exchange, you gain horizon and
perspective, leading you to clarity."
Dr. Bak Nguyen

1346
FROM 1SELF
"If you are more than you have, changing direction
to adapt to the flow of life should not be
that big of a challenge."
Dr. Bak Nguyen

1347
FROM ALPHA LADDERS VOLUME 2
"We all do, we change, we evolve.
How long will that ORDER stay relevant?"
Dr. Bak Nguyen

1348
FROM ALPHA LADDERS VOLUME 2
"Ambition is the motor of evolution, after surviving."
Dr. Bak Nguyen

1349
FROM ALPHA LADDERS VOLUME 2
"So ambition is good! It is what's driving the world."
Dr. Bak Nguyen

1350
FROM ALPHA LADDERS VOLUME 2
"The purpose of Life was to evolve and to adapt,
not to freeze the world within a picture
and to bonzai its growth."
Dr. Bak Nguyen

1351
FROM ALPHA LADDERS VOLUME 2
"Ambition is not bad. On the contrary,
it is a very powerful leverage when empowered."
Dr. Bak Nguyen

1352
FROM ALPHA LADDERS VOLUME 2
"The compassion to evolve with no resistance
and fewer collaterals, we are ready for that."
Dr. Bak Nguyen

1353
FROM ALPHA LADDERS VOLUME 2
"To Evolve is to Change. Change causes Resistance."
Dr. Bak Nguyen

1354
"Evolution is smooth without pride. The second part is obvious and yet so hard to achieve."
Dr. Bak Nguyen

1355
"Evolution is a lonely path."
Dr. Bak Nguyen

1356
"To be ready to be mentored is to accept to surrender our own insecurities."
Dr. Bak Nguyen

1357
"Evolution is a pain, the pain to change."
Dr. Bak Nguyen

1358
"The course of evolution eventually will divert from the path of happiness."
Dr. Bak Nguyen

1359

FROM MIRRORS

"When a student rebels from his teacher, it is often because the pain was higher than the foreseeable benefits."

Dr. Bak Nguyen

1360

FROM MIRRORS

"Even nature, in other words, God, has to try and fail to find balance."

Dr. Bak Nguyen

1361

FROM TO OVERACHIEVE EVERYTHING BEING LAZY

"With both our feet firmly planted in the past, the future is not that easily accessible. Even less changeable."

Dr. Bak Nguyen

1362

FROM TO OVERACHIEVE EVERYTHING BEING LAZY

"If an opportunity and a risk were both different faces of the same coin, challenge is the coin."

Dr. Bak Nguyen

1363

"The later one faces a challenge,
the great is the ratio risk/opportunity."

Dr. Bak Nguyen

1364

"We evolve, we do not change."

Dr. Bak Nguyen

This is **Shortcut volume 4, CONFIDENCE**. Welcome to the Alphas.

Dr. BAK NGUYEN

PART 5
"EMPOWERMENT"
by Dr. BAK NGUYEN

Empowerment, the day that I discovered that word, my life change 180 degrees. The first time that I really started using the word empowerment is when I was working on **EMOTIVE NOW**, my first internet endeavour, looking to decentralize power to keep the country united.

Fun fact, do you know that there is no equivalent word in the French language? I spent hours looking for its French translation but nothing even came close. So I guess that empowerment is a relatively new term. Encouragement was the word that was pointed to as translation.

"Encouragement is good but nothing
close to empowerment."
Dr. Bak Nguyen

Encouragement does not cost much to those who are giving it while empowerment comes with beliefs, support, and endorsement. In that sense to empower is also to add 2 spirits one on top of the other. This is where the power comes from.

It was really strange to me that empowerment was so hard to translate. To me, that concept existed for ages as each mentor is empowering their proteges, as each king is shaping their successors, as each parent is looking at their kids.

And that's when I realize that it was often more about power and being in control than to trust with power. That's what was missing in encouragement, there was no transfer of power!

"To empower, one must first be secure enough
to share and to open up."
Dr. Bak Nguyen

That's quote #2449. To empower, one must be secured enough to share power and generous enough to see beyond him or herself. To be empowered, one must first be grateful (to attract such generosity) and one must be mature enough to understand that the power received is lent, not given. Power is transitional and must serve a higher purpose.

That's the only way a greater mind would empower a younger one, with the hope of continuing his or her legacy. Like everything in life, empowerment is not free. But if both parties are ready, it is a great trade!

Until that point, as a father, I thought that I was empowering my son. I was encouraging him and boosting his **Confidence** with love and support but as a father, I was in control and did not understand the difference between encouragement and empowerment until I shared my powers and the control with him.

After setting the world record of writing 15 books within 15 months, I was exhausted. The last one, #015 was not an easy one to bring home. I was looking for a break. Then, William, my son of 8 reminded me that I promised to write a book with him. He was waiting for almost a year!

I felt really bad. As a man of my words, I would have kept my words with everyone but to my son?! So I did, we started writing our book the next day. I had no clue of what kind of book I was committing myself to, I just jump in and treated William as a partner. I shared my power of narrative and its control.

Well, what happened next made History. History will tell that to celebrate one world record, we scored 2 new ones, within a month!!! The following next 30 days, we wrote 8 children's books together as co-authors, as father and son. I was not his father, I was his partner!

I was empowering him to tell his story. He was empowering me to push forward with more intensity, ease, and energy. We broke the sound barrier, sort to speak, with such achievements. But much more, our connection and trust grew to another level. I grew to become his confidant and the person he comes to, to materialize his thoughts and ideas. He has learnt that if he can think it, it is possible.

"I will show you, I won't force you. But I won't wait for you."
William Bak & Dr. Bak Nguyen

That is a key signature quote that we found together. William will continue to write with me to reach a total of 27 books at the time of this writing. My point here is that empowerment works both ways.

My son elevated my game and pushed me to break the sound barrier, after that, I became a **tornado of productivity**. For my part, I did even more, boosting the skills and **Confidence** of an 8 years old to the ranks of speaker and motivator. If prior to writing with me, William was a shy speaker, within weeks, he became a natural orator.

The videos that we recorded while we were writing together and while we were in the *zone*, will show you the empowerment he received and the Confidence he developed. He might be born with some Confidence, empowerment gave him the opportunity to build up his own Confidence, one that Conformity cannot take away from him. And he was only 8. Can you imagine what he will be building if he is keeping that course?

That, in return, elevated me as *father of the year*, sort to speak! I was at the peak of my midlife crisis, I had huge problems at home. Well, thanks to William, we elevated each other above the **glass ceiling** and found other horizons to explore. From there, the drama dimmed down as I was not looking down or back. He knows it, he saved the family!

What about that for an empowerment story? And that is a true story. I will invite any of you with curiosity to read the franchise of **THE BOOK OF LEGENDS** to walk our journey in our footsteps. By the time of this writing, there are 3 volumes.

So to work, empowerment involves trust and the sharing of power. To do that, only a secured heart can empower. But then, if the recipient is open and mature enough to yield the power transferred to him or her, empowerment works both ways, sending much energy back to the sender. And just like in chemistry, the sum of energy produced is not the addition of the energy of both the parties involved but will result in a much greater explosion of energy.

That's **synergy** will propel each of the parties into their own momentum. Some will surf it to new heights, others will celebrate until the wave fades away. That's ok too since they now know how to create synergy, with **empowerment**!

This is also why I said that self-empowerment does not work. Before one has the privilege to have someone to share with (a mentor or a protege), one only has the *reflection* in the mirror to react to. That's fine, that's the beginning. I, myself, trained with my reflection for a long time.

The key is to stay open to welcome the arrival of either a mentor or a protege to mentor. And you know what? The more I am open, the more I attract, both mentors and proteges.

And what is best, to be a mentor or to be a protege? Well, Life has its way to balance. I had received as much from both ends. I learnt and grew much as a protege. I mastered and grew even more as I was mentoring. Both times, I grew from my actions and my reactions to the consequences. Having a mentor or a protege is giving the theme to the actions.

The only danger here is to know who you are receiving your advice and empowerment from. In the same line of thoughts, who you are empowering and believing in.

The wrong person will set you back and hurt you badly. That's the nature of empowerment, you are vulnerable as you are opening up. But because you are opening up, this is also how you have a chance to grow beyond your understanding.

This is **Shortcut volume 4, CONFIDENCE**. Welcome to the Alphas.

Dr. BAK NGUYEN

PART 6

"265 EMPOWERMENT QUOTES"

by Dr. BAK NGUYEN

1809
FROM FORCES OF NATURE
"That's how sex works, sometimes you're on top
and some other times, you are pinned down.
The pleasure is in the movement."
Dr. Bak Nguyen

1810
FROM THE BOOK OF LEGENDS, VOLUME 1
"If you want to live forever, try empathy of the youth."
Dr. Bak Nguyen

1811
FROM SELFMADE
"Emotion is the beast inside of us.
We can mount it or be eaten by it."
Dr. Bak Nguyen

1812
FROM SELFMADE
"Behind the walls, you will grow roots and thoughts,
but you've lost your horizon."
Dr. Bak Nguyen

1813
FROM SELFMADE
"Have the right mindset and you will redefine
your reality and the world with it."
Dr. Bak Nguyen

1814

FROM SELFMADE

"The fear of God keeps me going without hesitation."

Dr. Bak Nguyen

1815

FROM THE RISE OF THE UNICORN

"Never stand in the way of momentum,
especially yours."

Dr. Bak Nguyen

1816

FROM THE RISE OF THE UNICORN

"If pressure can stress, tension can be empowering!"

Dr. Bak Nguyen

1817

FROM THE RISE OF THE UNICORN

"Some need to shine. Some shine despite
themselves. Either way, it took something really
strong for you to notice."

Dr. Bak Nguyen

1818

FROM THE RISE OF THE UNICORN

"Be gracious, be grateful and do not have any
expectations but those you put upon yourself."

Dr. Bak Nguyen

1819

FROM THE RISE OF THE UNICORN

"Through structure and with a community,
I found both success and happiness."

Dr. Bak Nguyen

1820

FROM THE RISE OF THE UNICORN

"I play to win. If I don't, it's just a matter of time before
I find my leverage and come back victorious."

Dr. Bak Nguyen

1821

FROM THE RISE OF THE UNICORN

"The words will always resonate longer than guns…
That's the essence of hope over fear."

Dr. Bak Nguyen

1822

FROM THE RISE OF THE UNICORN

"Inspiration is when your intelligences aligned."

Dr. Bak Nguyen

1823

FROM THE RISE OF THE UNICORN

"To bet is to leverage and to have confidence in
oneself. Otherwise, it is a simple gamble…
and I don't gamble."

Dr. Bak Nguyen

1824

FROM THE RISE OF THE UNICORN

"I surfed the wave and mastered my skills.
Then, the wave became bigger, and I was ready."

Dr. Bak Nguyen

1825

FROM THE RISE OF THE UNICORN

"... I had to provoke things in my daily life to have
something worthwhile to write about!"

Dr. Bak Nguyen

1826

FROM THE RISE OF THE UNICORN

"Find the way to synergy, not jealousy."

Dr. Bak Nguyen

1827

FROM THE RISE OF THE UNICORN

"To win, find leverage from your emotions.
It is called to build Momentum."

Dr. Bak Nguyen

1827

FROM THE RISE OF THE UNICORN

"Timing is key for winning."

Dr. Bak Nguyen

1828

"To change, write down your resolution and share it."

Dr. Bak Nguyen

1829

FROM THE RISE OF THE UNICORN

"Writing without sharing holds very little power."

Dr. Bak Nguyen

1830

FROM THE POWER OF YES VOLUME TWO

"I went from sprinting to a marathon of sprints,
always speeding up and pushing forward,
a chapter at a time."

Dr. Bak Nguyen

1831

FROM THE POWER OF YES VOLUME TWO

"Yes, I am now a Yesman!"

Dr. Bak Nguyen

1832

FROM CHAMPION MINDSET

"Whoever thinks LIVE, thinks Selfie."

Dr. Bak Nguyen

1833

FROM CHAMPION MINDSET

"First, you adapt to survive, and then,
you stay open to thrive."

Dr. Bak Nguyen

1834

FROM CHAMPION MINDSET

"One will always have the mentor one deserves."

Dr. Bak Nguyen

1835

FROM CHAMPION MINDSET

"Run to your first fall, the sooner, the better!"

Dr. Bak Nguyen

1836

FROM CHAMPION MINDSET

"To win or to lose, it's a choice you made."

Dr. Bak Nguyen

1837

FROM CHAMPION MINDSET

"Align your emotions and your ambitions,
and nothing will stand in your way."

Dr. Bak Nguyen

1838
"Feel the glass half empty to keep your hunger
and your will to keep winning."

Dr. Bak Nguyen

1839
"Your narrative is not your identity; rather, your image
and name in the eyes of your audience."

Dr. Bak Nguyen

1840
"Your peers, your family, most of the people
who knew you from the beginning are hardly part
of your audience."

Dr. Bak Nguyen

1841
"To learn to leverage on a narrative will keep your
winning streak. Those who win time and time again
are those having the favour of the public."

Dr. Bak Nguyen

1842
FROM CHAMPION MINDSET
"Learn to edit your narrative into your legend."

Dr. Bak Nguyen

1843
FROM CHAMPION MINDSET
"Your narrative and your identity
are two different things."

Dr. Bak Nguyen

1844
FROM CHAMPION MINDSET
"Have a plan and see it through!"

Dr. Bak Nguyen

1845
FROM CHAMPION MINDSET
"You can have the best cards on the table and
the best skills, you still need chips to bet!"

Dr. Bak Nguyen

1846
FROM CHAMPION MINDSET
"There's a place for everyone;
you just need to find yours."

Dr. Bak Nguyen

1847

FROM CHAMPION MINDSET

"Your mentor will help you through the emotions
of your journey, not just the physical
and the intellectual."

Dr. Bak Nguyen

1848

FROM CHAMPION MINDSET

"Time is the essence of the trade between
a mentor and his protege."

Dr. Bak Nguyen

1849

FROM CHAMPION MINDSET

"Without leverage and momentum, you are hoping
to win with only the lower half of the deck."

Dr. Bak Nguyen

1850

FROM CHAMPION MINDSET

"Emotions are the real forces within each of us.
Learn to play and to dialogue with them."

Dr. Bak Nguyen

1851

"To feel the feeling of thriving and the win
on your face, you'll need momentum."

Dr. Bak Nguyen

1852

"The first rule of Momentum is to keep
the ball rolling."

Dr. Bak Nguyen

1853

"The second rule of momentum is to speed it up
as you feel the troubles coming your way."

Dr. Bak Nguyen

1854

"The third rule of Momentum is to look
for the next win, as small as it might be."

Dr. Bak Nguyen

1855

"To be able to keep your Momentum sane,
one needs to rest to refocus."

Dr. Bak Nguyen

1856

FROM CHAMPION MINDSET

"Everything about winning and leadership
is an opinion."

Dr. Bak Nguyen

1857

FROM CHAMPION MINDSET

"You cannot go further than what you can see."

Dr. Bak Nguyen

1858

FROM CHAMPION MINDSET

"All mentors will change and affect
the life of their proteges."

Dr. Bak Nguyen

1859

FROM CHAMPION MINDSET

"Whatever you believe will be."

Dr. Bak Nguyen

1860

FROM CHAMPION MINDSET

"If your beliefs and your own words might draft your
future, leave to the others to qualify your past."

Dr. Bak Nguyen

1861

FROM CHAMPION MINDSET

"Stay focus, and sooner or later,
success will come knocking."

Dr. Bak Nguyen

1862

FROM CHAMPION MINDSET

"You are and will be what you think."

Dr. Bak Nguyen

1863

FROM CHAMPION MINDSET

"Remember, you can't change the past,
but you are writing the future."

Dr. Bak Nguyen

1864

FROM CHAMPION MINDSET

"Be and feel, that's the champion in you talking."

Dr. Bak Nguyen

1865

FROM HOW TO WRITE A BOOK IN 30 DAYS

"From within, I found a way to escape,
to keep surfing my Momentum."

Dr. Bak Nguyen

1866

FROM HOW TO WRITE A BOOK IN 30 DAYS

"The real power of writing is when you are free to write your present and future, free from the past."

Dr. Bak Nguyen

1867

FROM HOW TO WRITE A BOOK IN 30 DAYS

"To write your first book as soon as possible frees you from your past."

Dr. Bak Nguyen

1868

FROM HOW TO WRITE A BOOK IN 30 DAYS

"Your freedom is waiting ahead.
Run to it with confidence."

Dr. Bak Nguyen

1869

FROM HOW TO WRITE A BOOK IN 30 DAYS

"To write a book is a dialogue."

Dr. Bak Nguyen

1870

FROM HOW TO WRITE A BOOK IN 30 DAYS

"To write is to relive a second time, differently and more completely."

Dr. Bak Nguyen

1871
"Know your audience; it is a sure way
to start your writing."

Dr. Bak Nguyen

1872
"Know your audience and establish a connection."

Dr. Bak Nguyen

1873
"Start with a win; it is easier."

Dr. Bak Nguyen

1874
"Structure will get your ideas into words,
words into sentences, and sentences into chapters."

Dr. Bak Nguyen

1875
"The introduction is the most important step of the
journey since it will set the tone for what's coming."

Dr. Bak Nguyen

1876

FROM HOW TO WRITE A BOOK IN 30 DAYS

"Consistency more than talent,
that's what it will take to write successfully."

Dr. Bak Nguyen

1877

FROM HOW TO WRITE A BOOK IN 30 DAYS

"Writing is an evolving process. It takes time."

Dr. Bak Nguyen

1878

FROM HOW TO WRITE A BOOK IN 30 DAYS

"The best empowerments are from within."

Dr. Bak Nguyen

1879

FROM HOW TO WRITE A BOOK IN 30 DAYS

"Chapters are the stones of your foundation.
With chapters, you'll build a journey."

Dr. Bak Nguyen

1880

FROM HOW TO WRITE A BOOK IN 30 DAYS

"As a writer, your most loyal allies are
structure and consistency."

Dr. Bak Nguyen

1881

"One chapter, one theme."

Dr. Bak Nguyen

1882

"If I have done it, so can you!"

Dr. Bak Nguyen

1883

"Write honestly and share boldly."

Dr. Bak Nguyen

1884

"Celebrate not with a break but
with a toast of Momentum!"

Dr. Bak Nguyen

1885

"Writing was the easiest part of the journey!"

Dr. Bak Nguyen

1886

"When I feel, I create. When I don't know, I observe."

Dr. Bak Nguyen

1887

"Changing the world with two thumbs,
that's surely a first! "

Dr. Bak Nguyen

1888

"I don't know when I will hit a wall, but until then,
I am having much fun writing, discovering,
and sharing with you."

Dr. Bak Nguyen

1889

"Eventually, writing will show you what's coming next,
since you wrote about it."

Dr. Bak Nguyen

1890

"Stay genuine and honest. Then, you can be bold!"

Dr. Bak Nguyen

1891

FROM HOW TO WRITE A BOOK IN 30 DAYS

"Writing is much about pace and timing."

Dr. Bak Nguyen

1892

FROM HOW TO WRITE A BOOK IN 30 DAYS

"Writing is about feeling much more than thinking.
Have people feel and they will think if you ask them.
Otherwise, we are all lazy."

Dr. Bak Nguyen

1893

FROM HOW TO WRITE A BOOK IN 30 DAYS

"I kept writing at a very frenetic pace, but
my state of mind was calm and smooth."

Dr. Bak Nguyen

1894

FROM HOW TO WRITE A BOOK IN 30 DAYS

"If you are bold, your actions will have
to be even bolder! The results, unfortunately,
are not just yours to control."

Dr. Bak Nguyen

1895

FROM THE BOOK OF LEGENDS, VOLUME 2
"Catching up is not a win.
To win, you must feel empowered, first!"
Dr. Bak Nguyen

1896

FROM THE BOOK OF LEGENDS, VOLUME 2
"Respect, that's the truth of life.
Respect and discover to understand and to master."
Dr. Bak Nguyen

1897

FROM THE BOOK OF LEGENDS, VOLUME 2
"Why should we be shy about something that we did?
If we did it, let's embrace it! "
Dr. Bak Nguyen

1898

FROM THE BOOK OF LEGENDS, VOLUME 2
"Trust yourself enough to embrace the unknown
and to follow your heart."
Dr. Bak Nguyen

1899

FROM THE BOOK OF LEGENDS, VOLUME 2

"A victory at a time, there won't be
any fear left eventually."

Dr. Bak Nguyen

1900

FROM THE BOOK OF LEGENDS, VOLUME 2

"Dreaming is like flying. You have to take
actions and learn to become better."

Dr. Bak Nguyen

1901

FROM THE BOOK OF LEGENDS, VOLUME 2

"You can outgrow your fears."

Dr. Bak Nguyen

1902

FROM THE BOOK OF LEGENDS, VOLUME 2

"Doubt will kill most dreams. To doubt,
that's in your head, not your heart."

Dr. Bak Nguyen

1903

FROM THE BOOK OF LEGENDS, VOLUME 2

"To create a Momentum, start to feel your heart.
And take the action it tells you to do."

Dr. Bak Nguyen

1904

FROM THE BOOK OF LEGENDS, VOLUME 2

"If I can write this much, it is because
my EMOTIONS and AMBITIONS are now aligned."

Dr. Bak Nguyen

1905

FROM POWER, EMOTIONAL INTELLIGENCE

"I was diving into my emotions.
My Momentum kept me afloat."

Dr. Bak Nguyen

1906

FROM POWER, EMOTIONAL INTELLIGENCE

"Feeling is information, nothing more
and nothing less."

Dr. Bak Nguyen

1907

FROM POWER, EMOTIONAL INTELLIGENCE

"Emotional Intelligence is a gift from God.
Why waste it?"

Dr. Bak Nguyen

1908

FROM POWER, EMOTIONAL INTELLIGENCE

"Align your emotions and your ambitions, and you are
unstoppable. Harmony is compelling."

Dr. Bak Nguyen

1909

FROM POWER, EMOTIONAL INTELLIGENCE

"Ride the crowd as you are surfing the waves.
Nothing last forever, nothing is stable.
But it can be fluid, though."

Dr. Bak Nguyen

1910

FROM POWER, EMOTIONAL INTELLIGENCE

"Act respectfully and gracefully; those are my secrets."

Dr. Bak Nguyen

1911

FROM POWER, EMOTIONAL INTELLIGENCE

"Respect them, love them, and make them love you!"

Dr. Bak Nguyen

1912

FROM POWER, EMOTIONAL INTELLIGENCE

"Don't try to help someone who doesn't want help. He will be fighting you through each step of the way, and you will be the villain of the story."

Dr. Bak Nguyen

1913

FROM POWER, EMOTIONAL INTELLIGENCE

"Words are strong and bold; actions must follow and beat the words."

Dr. Bak Nguyen

1914

FROM POWER, EMOTIONAL INTELLIGENCE

"Our tendency to cut everything into smaller parts to accommodate our understanding made us lose sight of the big picture and the whole."

Dr. Bak Nguyen

1915

"Greater than a skill or a craft, are respect
and awareness of oneself."

Dr. Bak Nguyen

1916

"I wanted to change the world. By circumstances,
almost by accident, I ended up changing it
a second time..."

Dr. Bak Nguyen

1917

"My honesty, boldness and naivety fused
into a new word: visionary."

Dr. Bak Nguyen

1918

"Don't just control the narrative, be the narrative!"

Dr. Bak Nguyen

1919

"Mark one's imagination and then,
surprise them by beating their expectation.
That's how you keep their interests."

Dr. Bak Nguyen

1920

FROM BRANDING

"Creativity is not something to command.
One only needs to be open when it comes knocking."

Dr. Bak Nguyen

1921

FROM BRANDING

"I changed the world from a dental chair,
I write books at a record pace, and I still have to
become a good dad and a man of my word."

Dr. Bak Nguyen

1922

FROM BRANDING

"My words and the crowd, that was it."

Dr. Bak Nguyen

1923

FROM BRANDING

"Momentum usually comes with a price, satisfaction and happiness."

Dr. Bak Nguyen

1924

FROM BRANDING

"Showing up, that's the first and most important step of the journey."

Dr. Bak Nguyen

1925

FROM HORIZON VOLUME ONE

"Think it, want it, make it happen!"

Dr. Bak Nguyen

1926

FROM HORIZON VOLUME ONE

"I care, I share, and I am done adapting to please."

Dr. Bak Nguyen

1927
FROM HORIZON VOLUME ONE
"Victors are too busy grinding to stop
and contemplate what they have accomplished.
Look at the horizon, that a breath and enjoy.
It will help to refocus and replenish before diving
back in."
Dr. Bak Nguyen

1928
FROM HORIZON VOLUME ONE
"Epiphany is one's realization of oneself.
Look forward to them."
Dr. Bak Nguyen

1929
FROM HORIZON VOLUME ONE
"We were literally standing in the land
of the DREAM IT and MAKE IT."
Dr. Bak Nguyen

1930
FROM HORIZON VOLUME ONE
"Influence reality with ease and without much
resistance, by smiling my way through life."
Dr. Bak Nguyen

1931
FROM HORIZON VOLUME ONE
"We are all the main character of our own story and a supporting or side character in someone else's story."
Dr. Bak Nguyen

1932
FROM HORIZON VOLUME ONE
"Live your life as a movie,
and you will be writing your legend."
Dr. Bak Nguyen

1933
FROM HORIZON VOLUME ONE
"Security and stability are the roots grounding
one to the ground. For a tree, that is great,
for a tornado, that will kill it."
Dr. Bak Nguyen

1934
FROM THE POWER OF YES, VOLUME 1
"Writing is really about focus and intensity."
Dr. Bak Nguyen

1935

FROM HORIZON VOLUME TWO

"I brought in the knowledge and experience
of movie making to this world of words.
That's how EAX came to life."

Dr. Bak Nguyen

1936

FROM HORIZON VOLUME TWO

"Writing, to me, is a way to have a conversation,
first, with my inner self."

Dr. Bak Nguyen

1937

FROM HOW TO NOT FAIL AS A DENTIST

"I prefer to be either climbing the mountain or skiing
downhill, at least, the mountain will be my support
and the wind, my ally."

Dr. Bak Nguyen

1938

FROM HOW TO NOT FAIL AS A DENTIST

"Be genuine and kind, you never know where
Life will lead you!"

Dr. Bak Nguyen

1939

FROM HOW TO NOT FAIL AS A DENTIST

"If money won't make your happiness, financial ignorance will doom you to a life of misery."

Dr. Bak Nguyen

1940

FROM HOW TO NOT FAIL AS A DENTIST

"The answers are all out there. You just have to open the door. If not out, then, as you open up, you will hear the answers within too!"

Dr. Bak Nguyen

1941

FROM HOW TO NOT FAIL AS A DENTIST

"There is a simple recipe to happiness and success: to listen to yourself truly."

Dr. Bak Nguyen

1942

FROM HOW TO WRITE A SUCCESSFUL BUSINESS PLAN

"To leverage your words into reality, it is sharing, not selling."

Dr. Bak Nguyen

1943

FROM HOW TO WRITE A SUCCESSFUL BUSINESS PLAN

"Logic will take many words to explain,
go for the emotions instead."

Dr. Bak Nguyen

1944

FROM HOW TO WRITE A SUCCESSFUL BUSINESS PLAN

"Forget perfection, just have a draft done and online
as quickly as possible. Then react and refine."

Dr. Bak Nguyen

1945

FROM HOW TO WRITE A SUCCESSFUL BUSINESS PLAN

"It is easier to scale down than to scale up.
While planning, leave room for the scaling down."

Dr. Bak Nguyen

1946

FROM HOW TO WRITE A SUCCESSFUL BUSINESS PLAN

"Make a stand and move forward from there,
never looking back."

Dr. Bak Nguyen

1947

FROM HOW TO WRITE A SUCCESSFUL BUSINESS PLAN

"Smile and readjust. It's a new day, it's a new game."

Dr. Bak Nguyen

1948
"Your best, but you, pure you!"

Dr. Bak Nguyen

1949
" Shoot for the moon, that's the best way
to minimize the risk/reward ratio. "

Dr. Bak Nguyen

1950
" Loyalty and transparency, those are the qualities
you need to show to seduce your bank."

Dr. Bak Nguyen

1951
"Emotions control Hormones.
Hormones control everything else."

Dr. Bak Nguyen

1952
"Control your emotions,
and you will master everything else!"

Dr. Bak Nguyen

1953

FROM MINDSET ARMORY

"Respect yourself, respect your environment, respect your tools."

Dr. Bak Nguyen

1954

FROM MINDSET ARMORY

"To be aware, that's the key to emotions."

Dr. Bak Nguyen

1955

FROM MINDSET ARMORY

"To rule the world, one must start by ruling oneself first."

Dr. Bak Nguyen

1956

FROM MINDSET ARMORY

"If you feel, you will believe. This is when things start to happen."

Dr. Bak Nguyen

1957

FROM MINDSET ARMORY

"Feel to believe and believe to achieve."

Dr. Bak Nguyen

1958

"Hope is the essence of a hero."

Dr. Bak Nguyen

1959

"GRATITUDE and GRACE will become the GENEROSITY and KINDNESS in the character as a hero."

Dr. Bak Nguyen

1960

"Nowadays, a sword is not meant to strike, but to serve as a beacon."

Dr. Bak Nguyen

1961

"Social accountability is the best fix to procrastination."

Dr. Bak Nguyen

1962
FROM MINDSET ARMORY
"By the time you have identified your haters,
you know that you are on the right path
to achieve something of worth!"

Dr. Bak Nguyen

1963
FROM MINDSET ARMORY
"The Shield I hold is not to protect myself,
but to connect with you."

Dr. Bak Nguyen

1964
FROM MINDSET ARMORY
"I exercise with them everyday, polishing them with
my experiences and ambitions. That's how the old
never gets old and the new has credibility."

Dr. Bak Nguyen

1965
FROM MINDSET ARMORY
"With generosity, awareness and openness,
there are no more doors close in this Universe."

Dr. Bak Nguyen

1966
FROM MINDSET ARMORY
"Only have an army to keep serving!"

Dr. Bak Nguyen

1967
FROM MINDSET ARMORY
"The higher the mountain, the larger its base,
the broader the horizon."

Dr. Bak Nguyen

1968
FROM MINDSET ARMORY
"Helping others was the only way I could feel
something real and meaningful in
a path that wasn't mine."

Dr. Bak Nguyen

1969
FROM MINDSET ARMORY
"Jealousy, we don't see. GREED we embrace
and FEAR, we leverage on."

Dr. Bak Nguyen

1970
FROM HUMILITY FOR SUCCESS
"I write my walks, those walks that I talked about."

Dr. Bak Nguyen

1971
"My Momentum allowed me stability and calm."
Dr. Bak Nguyen

1972
"You are not bragging, you are leveraging."
Dr. Bak Nguyen

1973
"The elasticity of the mind, the speed of adaptation
and the respect of the environment,
those are your leverage forward."
Dr. Bak Nguyen

1974
"A no is nothing, but the beginning of a new journey."
Dr. Bak Nguyen

1975
"That journey of your, if it is inspiring and retold,
it will become a legend."
Dr. Bak Nguyen

1976

FROM MASTERMIND

"Some times, it is better to record a loss and to digest it, than to keep the books open and not deal with the loss."

Dr. Bak Nguyen

1977

FROM MASTERMIND

"Every time I win, I am happy.
Every time I lose, I am motivated."

Dr. Bak Nguyen

1978

FROM MASTERMIND

"To build Momentum, build upon each win, as quickly as possible. If you need to replenish, do it while running."

Dr. Bak Nguyen

1979

FROM MASTERMIND

"The day I went out looking for Energy instead of money, time, or power, that day, I found all of them at my disposal."

Dr. Bak Nguyen

1980
FROM MASTERMIND
"Whatever you were seeking,
you will always find it inside."
Dr. Bak Nguyen

1981
FROM MASTERMIND
"To be open was one of my biggest success in my
journey. It brought power, fun and
legendary to the table."
Dr. Bak Nguyen

1982
FROM THE ENERGY FORMULA
"As an overachiever, solitude is your first companion."
Dr. Bak Nguyen

1983
FROM THE ENERGY FORMULA
"Hard work and discipline alone
are not enough to overachieve."
Dr. Bak Nguyen

1984
FROM THE ENERGY FORMULA
"Posting of social media is a way for me
to keep procrastination at bay."
Dr. Bak Nguyen

1985
FROM THE ENERGY FORMULA
"I am free of my choices, and I will walk the journey."
Dr. Bak Nguyen

1986
FROM THE ENERGY FORMULA
"I welcome, analyze, react and adapt."
Dr. Bak Nguyen

1987
FROM THE ENERGY FORMULA
"I am no victorious hero passing by.
I am just surfing through."
Dr. Bak Nguyen

1988
FROM THE ENERGY FORMULA
"I had so much going on that keeping track
was only to share, not to crystallize."
Dr. Bak Nguyen

1989
FROM THE ENERGY FORMULA
"Feel it, and it will be true."
Dr. Bak Nguyen

1990

"Energy is a pillar component of the universe,
it is universal. So is the Formula."

Dr. Bak Nguyen

1991

"My worse nightmare would be to wake up one day
and have nothing new to discover. That day,
the fun will have fade away…"

Dr. Bak Nguyen

1992

"Nobility is to leave more than we receive."

Dr. Bak Nguyen

1993

"Kindness is the key to Harmony. And Harmony,
the key to eliminate friction. From there, you will gain
infinite Speed, Power and Momentum."

Dr. Bak Nguyen

1994

"Be kind, so you can be King."

Dr. Bak Nguyen

1995

FROM PLAYBOOK INTRODUCTION VOLUME 1

"A new opportunity is often the biggest challenges you will have faced. Everything you achieve in your Life was leading you to that point.
Until the next one… "

Dr. Bak Nguyen

1996

FROM PLAYBOOK INTRODUCTION VOLUME 1

"The sooner you start, the lighter you are. Better your chance to reach a Momentum."

Dr. Bak Nguyen

1997

FROM PLAYBOOK INTRODUCTION VOLUME 1

"Tell me that I'll die tomorrow, I will simply speed up my pace to have as much accomplished before the end comes. "

Dr. Bak Nguyen

1998

FROM PLAYBOOK INTRODUCTION VOLUME 1

"It is never over until it is over!"

Dr. Bak Nguyen

1999

FROM PLAYBOOK INTRODUCTION VOLUME 2

"Helping and sharing with the youth is a chance
to live once more, once again.."

Dr. Bak Nguyen

2000

FROM PLAYBOOK INTRODUCTION VOLUME 2

"Find your essence, speed and Momentum
will follow."

Dr. Bak Nguyen

2001

FROM PLAYBOOK INTRODUCTION VOLUME 2

"People often think that experience and knowledge
is respected. Those can be stolen.
What they respect is resilience."

Dr. Bak Nguyen

2002

FROM SUCCESS IS A CHOICE

"To inspire, be genuine. to teach,
one has to be prepared."

Dr. Bak Nguyen

2003
FROM SUCCESS IS A CHOICE
"When you feel the heat, stopping will only burn you more. Speed up!"
Dr. Bak Nguyen

2004
FROM SUCCESS IS A CHOICE
"We have a chance to change our reality within the truth."
Dr. Bak Nguyen

2005
FROM SUCCESS IS A CHOICE
"Be the miracle worker, not the fixer."
Dr. Bak Nguyen

2006
FROM SUCCESS IS A CHOICE
"Nowadays, a person with credit is a rich person."
Dr. Bak Nguyen

2007
FROM SUCCESS IS A CHOICE
"Speed is the answer that you are looking for."
Dr. Bak Nguyen

2008

"Perspective will make make truth out of lies
and will render some truth eventually obsolete.
This is what we called a reality."

Dr. Bak Nguyen

2009

"We succeeded because we believed."

Dr. Bak Nguyen

2010

"Not everything is a march. sometimes
we have to dance too."

Dr. Bak Nguyen

2011

"To lose weight, one has to embrace losing
with a winner attitude."

Dr. Bak Nguyen

2012

"Fun leads to sustainability."

Dr. Bak Nguyen

2013
FROM RISING

"Success, abundance, wealth, happiness, they are all choices and perceptions of who we are within the world we chose to define."

Dr. Bak Nguyen

2014
FROM RISING

"To rise, open up and grow."

Dr. Bak Nguyen

2015
FROM RISING

"Do you want to win more than you are afraid to lose?"

Dr. Bak Nguyen

2016
FROM RISING

"If you can see beyond the clouds, you will see how small are your fears as you expand your horizon."

Dr. Bak Nguyen

2017
FROM RISING

"The WHY is a powerful motivator, but it is still in your mind and heart. Your hunger, that's visceral, much deeper and true to you."

Dr. Bak Nguyen

2018
FROM RISING

"Until you jump, you have no idea what it is nor what it involves."

Dr. Bak Nguyen

2019
FROM RISING

"So what you are willing to lose in order to win?"

Dr. Bak Nguyen

2020
FROM RISING

"You want to rise, do not stop nor look back."

Dr. Bak Nguyen

2021
"Speed became my power and Momentum,
my power animal."
Dr. Bak Nguyen

2022
FROM RISING
"Be bigger than your beliefs, by being
an insignificant part of the Universe."
Dr. Bak Nguyen

2023
FROM RISING
"Trade control for fun, and you will rise,
even despite yourself!"
Dr. Bak Nguyen

2024
FROM RISING
"You want to be rich, put your GREED in the service of
others. Ease theirs pains and treat theirs fears."
Dr. Bak Nguyen

2025
FROM RISING
"Rising is about making a statement. So is a million!"
Dr. Bak Nguyen

2026
FROM AFTERMATH
"In rare moments opportunity presents itself unannounced, grab it when it is there!"
Dr. Bak Nguyen

2027
FROM AFTERMATH
"Stay in the shadow and suffer the consequence of being left in line and being denied, forgotten."
Dr. Bak Nguyen

2028
FROM AFTERMATH
"I can afford to dilute my GREED, for as long as my vision can reach fructification."
Dr. Bak Nguyen

2029
FROM AFTERMATH

"The best leverages are the ones we put in place much before the facts, those we provoked and saw coming, not the one we have to react and improve on."
Dr. Bak Nguyen

2030
FROM AFTERMATH

"Philanthropy is not a dare nor a challenge, but leverage to matter."
Dr. Bak Nguyen

2031
FROM AFTERMATH

"Standing at the edge, I didn't ask myself what I had to lose, but how long I had to score another win…"
Dr. Bak Nguyen

2032
FROM AFTERMATH

"I listened with my heart, built with my GREED and executed leveraging from the differences."
Dr. Bak Nguyen

2033
FROM AFTERMATH

"On the tracks, we are unstoppable. At the GREAT PAUSE, we can now be unstoppable, even out of the tracks."

Dr. Bak Nguyen

2034
FROM RELEVANCY

"The time for half measures is over."

Dr. Bak Nguyen

2035
FROM RELEVANCY

"Now, we stand together from and with our diversity to face the common enemies, both from within: THE VIRUS and PRIDE."

Dr. Bak Nguyen

2036
FROM MIDAS TOUCH

"If it's natural, it won't be that hard!"

Dr. Bak Nguyen

2037

FROM MIDAS TOUCH

"Embrace your liability to make
them into your strength."

Dr. Bak Nguyen

2038

FROM MIDAS TOUCH

"We are on our own and we will stand tall!"

Dr. Bak Nguyen

2039

FROM TORNADO

"Building with only what you have in hand
will ground you to your present. Built with everything
you have in hand and look for more, but no need
to have planned accordingly."

Dr. Bak Nguyen

2040

FROM TORNADO

"Dragons exist, they are invisible since they change
shape all the time. That's the power of the dragon."

Dr. Bak Nguyen

2041
FROM EMPOWERMENT

"The only way for me to keep going is with fun…
and waiting, that's no fun at all."

Dr. Bak Nguyen

2042
FROM EMPOWERMENT

"Inspiration is motivation without resistance."

Dr. Bak Nguyen

2043
FROM EMPOWERMENT

"I defeat both resistance and pride with
one single word: empowerment."

Dr. Bak Nguyen

2044
FROM EMPOWERMENT

"That inner peace today is the core of my tornado,
a force of nature with the touch of a breeze."

Dr. Bak Nguyen

2045
"Another word for leveraging kindly
is empowerment."
Dr. Bak Nguyen

2046
"Respect, not justice. Harmony, not perfection.
Empowerment, not sacrifice."
Dr. Bak Nguyen

2047
"To please is not to empower."
Dr. Bak Nguyen

2048
"Empowerment and kindness will go along way."
Dr. Bak Nguyen

2049
"I am getting richer because I am getting wiser."
Dr. Bak Nguyen

2050
"Pleasing is not empowering, but it will buy you the time to understand one another."
Dr. Bak Nguyen

2051
FROM THE MODERN WOMAN
"Empowerment and kindness will go a long way."
Dr. Bak Nguyen

2052
FROM THE UAX STORY
"If you want to achieve something great, look for fun!"
Dr. Bak Nguyen

2053
FROM THE UAX STORY
"I will keep saying yes and keep surfing on the vibe of abundance, not waiting for permission and yes, I will be diluting the rejections."
Dr. Bak Nguyen

2054
FROM TOUCHSTONE, LEVERAGING TODAY'S PSYCHOLOGICAL SMOG
"I wrote 1.16 million words so you won't have to."
Dr. Bak Nguyen

2055

FROM TOUCHSTONE, LEVERAGING TODAY'S PSYCHOLOGICAL SMOG

"And in COVID times, fleeing is pretty limited.
So I decided to embrace a fourth alternative:
to leverage."
Dr. Bak Nguyen

2056

FROM ALPHA LADDERS VOLUME ONE

"The kind of talk that I empower are bold, vast,
and free. Walking these words takes more than
inspiration. It takes commitment."
Dr. Bak Nguyen

2057

FROM ALPHA LADDERS VOLUME ONE

"I am in it for the fun. I get my fun sharing
and scoring."
Dr. Bak Nguyen

2058

FROM ALPHA LADDERS VOLUME ONE

"Your WILL is not your desire, but the combination
of your experience, commitment,
and hunger for one thing."
Dr. Bak Nguyen

2059

FROM THE RISE OF THE UNICORN VOLUME TWO

"This time, friendship and respect got me
to the finished line."

Dr. Bak Nguyen

2060

FROM THE RISE OF THE UNICORN VOLUME TWO

"We are not imposing, we are simply empowering."

Dr. Bak Nguyen

2061

FROM THE RISE OF THE UNICORN VOLUME TWO

"Speed is the prime ingredient between hate and
envy, between jealousy and endorsement."

Dr. Bak Nguyen

2062

FROM THE RISE OF THE UNICORN VOLUME TWO

"This what eHappyPedia is about,
a shortcut to stardom."

Dr. Bak Nguyen

2063

FROM THE RISE OF THE UNICORN VOLUME TWO

"Not everyone will make it, but everyone will have a shot. It boils down to luck, mindset, and leverage."

Dr. Bak Nguyen

2064

FROM POWERPLAY

"Be a champion and you are running right into the hamster trap, the wheel of fortune!"

Dr. Bak Nguyen

2065

FROM ALPHA LADDERS VOLUME 2

"Empower ambition and you will release energy beyond understanding."

Dr. Bak Nguyen

2066

FROM ALPHA LADDERS VOLUME 2

"I share to heal. I share to feel. Then, I learn and I mastered. And to each word written, I need to deliver."

Dr. Bak Nguyen

2067

FROM THE BOOK OF LEGENDS VOLUME 3

"Empowerment is our gift to the world."

Dr. Bak Nguyen

2068

FROM THE BOOK OF LEGENDS VOLUME 3

"To plan is great, but actions have to follow quickly to not falls into burdens. So are expectations versus the amazement."

Dr. Bak Nguyen

2069

FROM THE CONFESSION OF AN OVERACHIEVER

"You cannot aim to overachieve trying to overachieve. It's all about growing."

Dr. Bak Nguyen

2070

FROM THE CONFESSION OF AN OVERACHIEVER

"Achieving will have their attention. Overachieving will mark their imagination."

Dr. Bak Nguyen

2071

"Yes, Humility and Confidence can co-exist!"

Dr. Bak Nguyen

2072

"Are you leveraging your fear or desires,
it is for you to choose."

Dr. Bak Nguyen

2073

"To uncover manipulation, amplify.
In every day's terms, empower people."

Dr. Bak Nguyen

This is **Shortcut volume 4, CONFIDENCE**. Welcome to the Alphas.

Dr. BAK NGUYEN

PART 7

"THE POWER OF QUOTES"

by Dr. BAK NGUYEN

I can't believe how easy it is to move forward jumping from quotes to quotes. Earlier, I said that I can do today, in a day, what took me a year to achieve before. Well, reading and growing from quotes to quotes and with the mapping of my entire library, one can go through the evolution within days instead of months.

Even writing this book felt the same. There is always that feeling of overwhelming and that temptation of procrastination and laziness but once I lay the first words of a chapter, the rest follows effortlessly. That is how it feels like to be in **the zone**.

One can only be in the zone as one is calm and open to merge with the **frequency of the universe**. And calm, we covered that already, to be calm, one needs to be secured, confident. And this is what this journey is about, to find your Confidence.

If you do anything daily, repeating the action day in and day out, it is simply a matter of time before you will see the result (consequences) of your actions. So it is, with doubting and feeding ourselves with wrong wording.

This is how education, training, and religion operate, through repetition and reinforcement. We too can benefit from that kind of reinforcement, 3 quotes a day, just like taking a pill. 3 quotes each day for 365 days. Some will be obvious while others might stay on your mind for days before you have your **aha moment**!

This is really what it is about, to break down the wealth and knowledge of an entire library so it can fit in our consumption habits. We are too busy to read. Fine, 3 quotes a day is easy, you will be asking for more!

We are busy and do not have time. 3 quotes will take you less than a minute to read, You can do that by waking up before starting your day, or in bed before closing your eyes for the night. The idea is to go through the wording and slowly, you will feel the journey already behind you.

Yes, what is covered in the 8 books of the **SHORTCUT** series is that universal quest that we all must walk alone. Within the shape of a quote, 3 at a time, you just have enough to leverage yourself through your day, through the challenge ahead.

And repetition? Well, I don't know many people who read the same book twice. I did, but that was exceptional. Knowing that mastering is coming with repetitions, how can a book help? A book, maybe not but a quote is a format that can leverage the **repetition process** daily.

More than random quotes, the **SHORTCUT** series have been compiled with the logic of guiding you through your journey, so each quote complements the last one and the next one. There is a logical process and a natural rise as you are moving forward. All you have to do is to read and think about 3 quotes a day. Not bad for a life-changing event, no?!

This is **the power of quotes**. Just like the previous volumes, coming next are the development of 8 of my 77 famous quotes, the core of my growth and power. These quotes vary from one volume to the next, in order to cover as much ground as possible.

I will explain and share with you shortly their story, 8 at a time, respecting the number of the Dragon. May they inspire you and find their use in the palm of your hands.

0003
FROM LEADERSHIP, PANDORA'S BOX
"One's legend can only begin the day one's
Quest of Identity is over."
Dr. Bak Nguyen

This might be my greatest finding. It is easy to understand if you refer to the Pyramid of Maslow.

SELF-ACTUALIZATION
ESTEEM
LOVE/BELONGING
SAFETY
PHYSIOLOGICAL NEEDS

THE PYRAMID OF ABRAHAM MASLOW

As you are looking to feed and secure your basic needs (physiological and safety, those are in a straight line between satisfaction and evolution), you arrive at the middle of the pyramid at **LOVE** and **BELONGING**. We all need love and we are all, at least at some point in our lives, looking to belong.

Well, everything until that point could be learnt from **Society** and **Conformity**. From them, we got our recipes and templates that were custom made to fit in society. This is also where we will break our nose on the *glass ceiling*.

But once we got through, leaving belong and peer pressure behind, we can then, rise from the average to our Destiny, our nature-given preferences. To find your identity is the journey of healing and to learn to listen to your inner voice.

You will be dealing with doubt and looking to give a voice to your natural Confidence, what you feel is right. The toughness part is to break from the *ranks of Conformity*, to *discount* our roots, and to march alone, isolated.

But once you have felt your first real victory, one without the crowd nor the medals, one that only you notice, you are building up your real Confidence, the kind that no one can take away from you. What will you do? Well, you will do it again and again. At each win, you a building your Confidence up, layer after layer.

All these wins are not from nowhere, there are because you made a difference for someone in need. This is how you are walking your legend, even before you realize that you were walking that path. To you, it was just getting to your next win, as soon as possible.

You have passed through the **glass ceiling**, looking for purpose, purpose not reassurance. That you might never task again since, on the journey that you are travelling, you are often alone to understand your path. On the other hand, you will be giving much comfort and reassurance to those you helped.

Growth happens at the giving end. You have the perfect deal in hand! So heal and grow, grow to go to your legend.

FAMOUS QUOTE 2

0016
FROM CHANGING THE WORLD FROM A DENTAL CHAIR
"Confidence is sexy."
Dr. Bak Nguyen

I signed that quote as I was trying to untie the last remnants of doubt and need for reassurance. Over the years, I achieved many exploits to be recognized universally as an overachiever. I have the mindset and the results to prove my point. And yet, many people did not like me, even when I have done nothing to them.

I usually don't stand in a crowd or within a group. When I started my reboot and learnt to open up and to get rid of judgment, I embarked on a journey saying **YES** to virtually everything for 18 months. I say virtually because I protected myself from making illegal or financial decisions while under the **INFLUENCE OF YES**.

Well, I tried very hard to fit in, to be accepted. People welcome my presence, even if they did not like me. Then, it was a matter of testing me to my limits, looking to see how far they can push. They did not know about my challenge but somehow my presence alone was pushing them to act as such.

Quickly, I learnt to recognize the face of jealousy. I shrugged my shoulders and move on. I was not the one with the problem, they were. It was not about me... and this is where I was wrong. It was all about me! What I am, they felt it. My Confidence and my strength, they all felt it and were intimidated by them.

Usually, when you see someone confident and powerful coming, you are covering your ass to make sure that you are not showing any sign of weakness. Well, I wasn't but people, especially weak people, and small minds often confuse kindness and generosity for weakness. That I learnt all too well.

And I was often alone, far from my troops and title. How could I intimidate them? I am 5 feet 6, and struggling with an overweight problem since I've graduated from dental school (Stress management). How could I intimidate tall and athletic guys? How could I intimidate successful orators and politicians? I intimidate them because I was Confident.

Even with the women, that got me ahead, much ahead. As a man, I have spent part of my life looking to be James Bond. Don't laugh, you did that too! Well, that never brought me much successes. One day, I looked in the mirror and acknowledged the person looking back at me. That was no James Bond. The person I saw looking back at me was Shrek!

Well, the day that I accept to be a Shrek instead of a James Bond, my charisma with the ladies went to the roof! Really, Confidence is sexy, once you get rid of the **wannabe phase** and of the doubts.

Confidence is calm. Confidence does not look for reassurance, proof nor looking to convince. You just are. And why do the ladies love confidence? Because only once confident can one really give and be generous. Confidence is sexy!

FAMOUS QUOTE 3

0024
FROM HYBRID
"Look for your next immediate win."
Dr. Bak Nguyen

We are in a race against time. False. We are in a race to keep our distance from doubt. Everything new and of worth that you are doing, no one can tell what will be the outcome, only you might feel it. You feel it but you don't know. To feel is within your heart or even deeper, within your guts. Thinking is in your head. And thinking is slow.

So as you are moving fast, your body will feel the speed and respond with the right hormones. Your heart will be pumping blood faster and faster to feed your body. It too will react accordingly with your actions. Only your mind may trick you here.

Move fast and your mind (which is always the slowest) will catch only glimpses of reality. It will kick in survival mode and analyze and process only the information you need to keep moving. Your mind is serving you well.

Slow down and let your mind have the time to record more data. Unless you are fully Confident, possibilities and alternatives will start to emerge. Then, you will be talking to people. Even more possibilities and stories will emerge. You are growing roots to map the field.

Well, the longer you stay in that phase, the harder it will be for you to resume your journey, walking your legend. Remember how it felt like under the **glass ceiling** as you knew that you were born for more, for better and the pain it took to break free from the ranks? Well, you are repeating yourself, the pain and the doubts part.

I don't know about you but I am too lazy to go through that phase twice. That is why I am surfing from one win to the next as quickly as possible. It is my best chance to beat doubt and to keep the energy flowing in the right direction, surfing, not walking!

For those of you who are still not convinced, I will urge you to read the **ENERGY FORMULA**, my 53rd book. You will find all the explanations that you seek.

Moving from win to win also has the advantage of feeding my body with the right hormones and keeping my heart hot and pumping.

Run a kilometre and see how your mind starts unclouding. I am serious, try it and tell me how it feels. Move to your next win as quickly as possible, before your mind can catch up and understand who you have become.

FAMOUS QUOTE 4

0055

FROM PLAYBOOK INTRODUCTION VOLUME 2

"Be careful since doubts is a pet that you are feeding."

Dr. Bak Nguyen

This one is obvious but I like the imagery so much. For those thinking that doubt will keep you alive, you are right. For those thinking that doubt will kill more of your dreams than your worse enemy, you are also right. For those thinking that doubt is a lie and that it has no effect on you, you will be right eventually.

Well, this is the power of our body, we can make what we believe into reality. This is no BS nor sorcery. In medicine, there is a famous phenomenon call **the placebo effect**.

The placebo effect stipulates that if the mind believes that something is true, it will react as such. Since what we are feeling is the hormonal response of our body to the exterior stimulus, to us, the feeling is real and genuine.

If you think that a ghost is standing behind you, you will be sacred. You will feel scared and not just in your head but your entire body will react as such. Your hair will be dressing up, you will feel a coldness and even a chill through out your body.

You are not fooling yourself, you are really feeling each of these sensations because your body produced these hormones in response to what it thought was real.

So in medicine, some people will heal from all of the symptoms even if the pills they took were sugar and food colouring. In the same line of thoughts, some people will be taking the real pill and won't heal at all. What you believe is having a huge impact on the outcome. And this is science, not folklore.

So whatever you believe, you are right. Take that **law of physiology** and add it up with the **law of repetition** and you will understand why some will never be happy. Choose your wording and your entourage carefully, they are the pills and repetition.

FAMOUS QUOTE 5

0058
FROM AMONGST THE ALPHAS, VOLUME 2
"Growth happens at the giving end,
not the receiving one."
Dr. Bak Nguyen

I absolutely adore this one because it is so true. I will love to say noble too but I can't, knowing that giving, I am the one growing more. That is not selflessness... but who cares? The result is the same, you are being generous and giving to people.

They will feed and heal. They might come back, make sure that you are gone and nowhere to be found. Giving once, you are kind. Giving to the same people, again and again, you are enslaving them. I learnt that one, giving and growing. I got bitten too.

Only once you are truly Confident can you forget yourself to give freely, genuinely. And then, what happens? You will be looking to find more of what you gave. That mindset and that insurance will propel you to your next quest. Keep moving from win to win and you are growing in **Abundance** with a capital A.

Your Confidence, your skills, your insurance to know that there is more ahead, those will push you to grow beyond your limits until you finally fade away the word from your lexicon…

That's on the giving end. What about the receiving end? I did receive much from God, from Life, from those who love me. The first thing to be is to be grateful and to honour those who are giving to you.

Then, consider what you've just received as a debt. Make the most of it and make sure that you are eating the profit, not the core. Only then, you won't be victim to the addiction of receiving.

Receive with grace and gratefulness and deliver on what you have received, as quickly as possible before doubt catches up with you and ties you down with questions and possibilities.

"Roots are always painful to cut."
Dr. Bak Nguyen

That's quote #2450. One last thing on the matter of giving. A sacrifice is no giving: a sacrifice happens when one has his or her back against the wall and does not have any more time to find a better alternative.

I won't be qualifying a sacrifice but what I can tell you is that if you are alert and see things far on your Horizon, the odds are that you won't be faced with the dilemma of giving for the last time.

Be proactive and smart and you won't have to debate sacrifice.

0066

FROM AFTERMATH
"Yes, we can have it all!"
Dr. Bak Nguyen

We talked briefly about **Abundance**. You now know that abundance is a state of mind that refuses to accept scarcity. In other words, if the food is running out here, one needs to expand his or her horizon to find more food. Either by expanding the field physically or by looking at different alternatives of food. In both cases, it was about expanding one's mind.

I also told you that whatever you think, you are right! This is the perfect example to illustrate that mindset. If you are convinced that there is no other solution, you are giving up.

You will accept to do and to be with lesser and your mind and body will react as such. Your mind will be busy rationalizing and finding a way to cope with the new reality.

Your body, a little like a frustrated child, will scream and scream to convince you that you need to find more food. It will make you feel the need miserably for the first hours, even days.

The feeling will be so bad that it might traumatize you. But you won't die from that pain. Then, it will respond is such to adapt to the new scarcity. You have just broken your spirit.

If you were doing that to lose weight and to break a bad circle, you were in control, so you did win. Otherwise, you are self-amputating your horizons and possibilities.

What I learnt is that for as long as you are looking up, you move up and you are moving in the direction of **Abundance**. As soon as you are looking down, everything changes drastically. And here they are waiting for you, **Doubts** and **Scarcity**.

Whatever you think, you are right! Keep this one close to your mind.

0070
FROM ALPHA LADDERS VOLUME ONE
"All good things start with a YES."
Dr. Bak Nguyen

As cheesy as it might sound, **Abundance** I found where I did not know existed. Read that again and you will see the image clearly. So? You thought that it was scarce because I did not look elsewhere. This is pure logic.

Abundance, happiness, and generosity often come together. Now that we know that the key to generosity leading to growth and abundance is from Confidence, we now know the way to Abundance, perhaps even Happiness.

And how do you grow Confidence? By finding your worth giving and serving others. This is how you grow the quickest and with the least resistance.

So start giving and replenish. Replenish faster than you are giving and you will have outgrown yourself, you will have evolved to the next level.

And what is giving but saying YES? You can give your time, your food, your energy, your skills. Whatever you give, make sure to replenish it even faster. To avoid resistance, I even gave my formula of replenishing, so I did not have a target in my back nor have to deploy many resources in the protection of a treasure.

I like shrines and oasis. I like mountains, beaches, and oceans, I want nothing to do with protection and secrets. So I gave mine away, I shared most of my findings. Doing so, I grew to become a world record writer finding even more powers than the one I gave away. That's how I made **EMPOWERMENT** my cornerstone.

And that started by saying **YES**. 18 months of this cure and what I gained is that I drop judging completely. Well, the first person I stop judging was myself. That day I gained the power of 3 me, just by dropping the judgment of both myself and the others. It is just like a lot of noise and dust suddenly disappear.

FAMOUS QUOTE 8

0076

FROM TO OVERACHIEVE EVERYTHING BEING LAZY

"I told you that everything in life is a trade.
Be careful of what you are trading."

Dr. Bak Nguyen

Nothing is ever free. Even when you are receiving freely, if you are not making up for what you have received, you will be paying the price growing fat and losing both your skills and potentials. This is on top of, that in Life, nothing is free, there is always a price to everything.

I learnt that since my childhood. To have what I wanted, I could either scream until people give me what I want. That only works with those who love you, until they grew afraid and are running from you. Quite a high price to pay to eat, don't you think?

My parents are immigrants, I did not even have that opinion to scream. Very quickly, I learnt to leverage and to trade in order to obtain what I want. I grew better and better in the art of trading.

The best deals that I found were not the ones where I give you something in exchange of something of equal value. The best deals were the ones where I gave more than I received. At least, I received, and usually very quickly. Now, it was for me to deliver.

I learnt at a very young age to overdeliver and to overachieve. That was, and still is, my best course of action to obtain what I desire. Slowly what I desired was more and more growth. I had the perfect recipe for that kind of hunger.

The idea is to always keep yourself on your toes to keep replenishing and to keep moving in **Abundance**. The only way that I found was through **Growth**, through **Confidence**, through **Generosity**.

Today and I power, abundant and generous because only those with the same mindset are still in my environment. Even those with different mindsets that I cherish, I found a common ground to evolve with them, with **Gratitude**. And you know that Gratitude is the only past with a future.

I trade to grow. I trade quickly to keep my pace and my speed. I will trade my time very carefully. Carefully, not with doubt nor indecision. I also always look for trades where the other party value something that I don't. That's the perfect deal, the one making everyone happy.

Well, I learnt that trading in the stock market. The world is vast and the people are diverse. Don't judge them and you just found more people to trade with.

This is **Shortcut volume 4, CONFIDENCE**. Welcome to the Alphas.

Dr. BAK NGUYEN

PART 8

"FAMOUS QUOTES"

by Dr. BAK NGUYEN

0001

FROM SYMPHONY OF SKILLS

"The pain of the problem has to be greater than the pain of change."

Dr. Bak Nguyen

0002

FROM SYMPHONY OF SKILLS

"Sharing is the way to grow."

Dr. Bak Nguyen

0003

FROM LEADERSHIP, PANDORA'S BOX

"One's legend can only begin the day one's Quest of Identity is over."

Dr. Bak Nguyen

0004

FROM IDENTITY, ANTHOLOGY OF QUESTS

"Gratitude is the only past with a future."

Dr. Bak Nguyen

0005

FROM PROFESSION HEALTH

"Mine was, forgive yourself."

Dr. Bak Nguyen

0006
"To walk on thin ice is a dangerous game.
To run is safer. To surf is the easiest."
Dr. Bak Nguyen

0007
"If I have changed the world from a dental chair,
you are all in a better position than I am
to change the world."
Dr. Bak Nguyen

0008
"The day you are fighting to raise the average instead
of beating it, that day, you've joined the leadership."
Dr. Bak Nguyen

0009
"At the end of the day, business is communication."
Dr. Bak Nguyen

0010
"Make leverage of each of your liabilities,
and you will always be moving forward."
Dr. Bak Nguyen

0011
FROM INDUSTRIES' DISRUPTORS
"I believe in myself and I do it for God,
not the other way around."
Dr. Bak Nguyen

0012
FROM INDUSTRIES' DISRUPTORS
"Always choose the path of least resistance."
Dr. Bak Nguyen

0013
FROM INDUSTRIES' DISRUPTORS
"Be mindful of the consequences."
Dr. Bak Nguyen

0014
FROM CHANGING THE WORLD FROM A DENTAL CHAIR
"Hammering air three times over and
it will become steel."
Dr. Bak Nguyen

0015

"Mdex, for joy for life."

Dr. Bak Nguyen

0016

"Confidence is sexy."

Dr. Bak Nguyen

0017

"Make it happen!"

Dr. Bak Nguyen

0018

FROM THE POWER BEHIND THE ALPHA

"Humility is to know what you are and to recognize what you are not."

Dr. Bak Nguyen

0019

FROM MOMENTUM TRANSFER

"On thin ice, speed up, that's how you will eventually learn to fly! "

Dr. Bak Nguyen

0020
FROM MOMENTUM TRANSFER
"Control with wisdom is called influence."
Dr. Bak Nguyen

0021
FROM MOMENTUM TRANSFER
"To stabilize a momentum, speed up!"
Dr. Bak Nguyen

0022
FROM HYBRID
"Chords and patterns are the themes of the Universe."
Dr. Bak Nguyen

0023
FROM HYBRID
"A weakness is a strength out of reach."
Dr. Bak Nguyen

0024
FROM HYBRID
"Look for your next immediate win."
Dr. Bak Nguyen

0025
FROM REBOOT, TO GROW FROM MIDLIFE CRISIS

"Don't stop the flow of a river unless you are ready to clean up the flood."

Dr. Bak Nguyen

0026
FROM LEVERAGE COMMUNICATION INTO SUCCESS

"Find your worth in the service of others."

Dr. Bak Nguyen

0027
FROM LEVERAGE COMMUNICATION INTO SUCCESS

"Humility is not the denial of oneself but the acceptance of one true nature."

Dr. Bak Nguyen

0028
FROM THE BOOK OF LEGENDS, VOLUME 1

"We are all born little, as a chicken heart. If we keep an open mind, we will grow into a lion heart. Some will choose to be close-minded and will remain small."

Dr. Bak Nguyen

0029

FROM THE BOOK OF LEGENDS, VOLUME 1

"To have an open mind is step one.
To keep growing, one needs an open heart."

Dr. Bak Nguyen

0030

FROM THE BOOK OF LEGENDS, VOLUME 1

"Humility is the ability to recognize and to respect
what we are, and stop pretending to be
what we are not."

Dr. Bak Nguyen

0031

FROM SELFMADE

"Good things start to happen when you say yes!"

Dr. Bak Nguyen

0032

FROM SELFMADE

"Knowledge is the ground of the past.
Hope and Dreams are the air of the future."

Dr. Bak Nguyen

0033

FROM SELFMADE

"My deepest fear is to show up before God
and not have enough to show for."

Dr. Bak Nguyen

0034

FROM THE RISE OF THE UNICORN

"To make the world a better place."

Dr. Bak Nguyen

0035

FROM THE RISE OF THE UNICORN

"A Momentum is when it is easier
to keep moving than to stop."

Dr. Bak Nguyen

0036

FROM CHAMPION MINDSET

"I was open, and I bet on myself."

Dr. Bak Nguyen

0037

FROM HOW TO WRITE A BOOK IN 30 DAYS

"To keep Momentum, aim for the next win,
as little as it might be."

Dr. Bak Nguyen

0038

FROM HOW TO WRITE A BOOK IN 30 DAYS

"A quote is a truth from another life,
from a past legacy."

Dr. Bak Nguyen

0039
FROM HOW TO WRITE A BOOK IN 30 DAYS
"The fewer the words, the better."

Dr. Bak Nguyen

0040
FROM POWER, EMOTIONAL INTELLIGENCE
"Align your emotions and your ambitions
to be whole, to be unstoppable."

Dr. Bak Nguyen

0041
FROM POWER, EMOTIONAL INTELLIGENCE
"I believe in myself, and I do it for God,
not the other way around."

Dr. Bak Nguyen

0042
FROM BRANDING
"I kept the "Dr." on to remind me to always
put your interests before mine."

Dr. Bak Nguyen

0043
FROM BRANDING
"Arrogance is not the bragging of our knowledge,
but rather the denial of our ignorance."

Dr. Bak Nguyen

0044

FROM HORIZON VOLUME ONE

"I treat people, not teeth."

Dr. Bak Nguyen

0045

FROM THE POWER OF YES, VOLUME 1

"Writing books allowed me to evolve at the speed of my thoughts."

Dr. Bak Nguyen

0046

FROM THE POWER OF YES, VOLUME 1

"Speed is my power. Momentum, my expression."

Dr. Bak Nguyen

0047

FROM THE POWER OF YES VOLUME 3

"We do not need to choose, only to prioritize."

Dr. Bak Nguyen

0048

FROM HOW TO NOT FAIL AS A DENTIST

"Changing the world from a dental chair."

Dr. Bak Nguyen

0049

"I am not giving up, I am simply wising up!"

Dr. Bak Nguyen

0050

"With your money, do not trust anyone but yourself."

Dr. Bak Nguyen

0051

"Reading will be cool again!"

Dr. Bak Nguyen

0052

"Until it is done, it is air, good air but only air."

Dr. Bak Nguyen

0053

"You can cheat, legally, by learning about shortcuts and leveraging."

Dr. Bak Nguyen

0054

FROM PLAYBOOK INTRODUCTION VOLUME 1

"Nothing will last forever, and nothing is free."

Dr. Bak Nguyen

0055

FROM PLAYBOOK INTRODUCTION VOLUME 2

"Be careful since doubts is a pet
that you are feeding."

Dr. Bak Nguyen

0056

FROM PLAYBOOK INTRODUCTION VOLUME 2

"Reach for your next win as soon as possible,
and build on it!"

Dr. Bak Nguyen

0057

FROM AMONGST THE ALPHAS, VOLUME 2

"Be bold, confident, and humble."

Dr. Bak Nguyen

0058

FROM AMONGST THE ALPHAS, VOLUME 2

"Growth happens at the giving end,
not the receiving one."

Dr. Bak Nguyen

0059
"Be bold, be flexible, act fast and stay humble."
Dr. Bak Nguyen

0060
"To succeed, be flexible."
Dr. Bak Nguyen

0061
"In times of crisis, one has to reinvent oneself."
Dr. Bak Nguyen

0062
"To matter, serve."
Dr. Bak Nguyen

0063
"There is no free money."
Dr. Bak Nguyen

0064
"For the first time of our lifetime,
all the interests of the world are aligned."
Dr. Bak Nguyen

0065

FROM AFTERMATH

"In times of crisis, it is the perfect opportunity to reinvent who we are. "

Dr. Bak Nguyen

0066

FROM AFTERMATH

"Yes, we can have it all!"

Dr. Bak Nguyen

0067

FROM TORNADO

"History will say that to celebrate one world record, we scored two more!"

Dr. Bak Nguyen

0068

FROM TORNADO

"The only way to keep overdelivering is playing, all-in!"

Dr. Bak Nguyen

0069

FROM TORNADO

"Dream and the means will come."

Dr. Bak Nguyen

0070

FROM ALPHA LADDERS VOLUME ONE

"All good things start with a YES."

Dr. Bak Nguyen

0071

FROM ALPHA LADDERS VOLUME 2

"Growth occurs at the giving end, always."

Dr. Bak Nguyen

0072

FROM THE CONFESSION OF AN OVERACHIEVER

"Being lazy doesn't mean that you don't have to do shit, it means that you don't have to go through shit to get things done."

Dr. Bak Nguyen

0073

FROM TO OVERACHIEVE EVERYTHING BEING LAZY

"Arrogance is not the recognition of who we are but the denial of what we are not."

Dr. Bak Nguyen

0074

"You call me doctor to remind me to always put your needs before mine."

Dr. Bak Nguyen

0075

"Nowadays, influence is power without liability."

Dr. Bak Nguyen

0076

"I told you that everything in life is a trade. Be careful of what you are trading."

Dr. Bak Nguyen

0077

"Fear is a disease and it must be treated like one."

Dr. Bak Nguyen

This is **Shortcut volume 4, CONFIDENCE**. Welcome to the Alphas.

Dr. BAK NGUYEN

CONCLUSION
by Dr. BAK NGUYEN

Wow, this is another step in the journey of **SHORTCUT**, of hacking our way to **SUCCESS, POWER**, and **HAPPINESS**. This journey took 2 days to be completed. And yet, it felt so natural and genuine. I will never have guessed that to make sense of my knowledge, I needed to find a cheat.

Well, I may be fooled myself looking for this cheat but I am so glad of how things turned out. Just like I said that everything starts with a **YES**, I said **YES** to myself and dealt with the consequences.

I am in the preparation and writing of the 8 books of **SHORTCUTS** for the last 2 months. The **SHORTCUT** series will not be a trilogy but a *Dragonology*, 8 books. I am halfway through with the completion of this one, **CONFIDENCE**, the fourth volume of **SHORTCUT**.

Writing **CONFIDENCE**, I made sure to summarize briefly the main concepts of **HEALING**, of **GROWING**, of **GIVING,** so you can follow the logic. Yes, the volumes are adding up but since I promised you a *hack*, I am keeping my words until the end. Even if that meant that I have to write more words…

In **CONFIDENCE**, we resume exactly where volume 3 left, **GIVING**. From there, we understood **EMPOWERMENT** and its difference with encouragement. And from **EMPOWERMENT** we simply exploded the growth potential through time and space.

An explosion that brought us to the doors of **ABUNDANCE** Not bad at all for a hack, no? So what's next? I started this chapter with them, **SUCCESS**, **POWER**, and **HAPPINESS** are the next three volumes of the *dragonology*. But don't rush Take the time to inhale and to let what you've learnt in this journey, to give it a change to sink in before rushing ahead. I told you to move fast, not to rush.

CONFIDENCE is by far the most complete and wise volume of the **SHORTCUT** series so far. How can I beat this one, I don't know. But I will, rest assured! I told you that **LEADERSHIP** was just the beginning of **RISING** and rising is the best part!

CONFIDENCE, what a key, what a mindset, what a powerful concept! That alone can make or break hearts, people, countries, empires, **CONFIDENCE**. With confidence, you are now in possession of your best tool to expand your heart and to be ready to harness more powers coming ahead.

Each new power, just like a wild horse, will try to run you first. The only way to face each of them is with

Confidence. That they respect, Confidence. Find yours and enjoy your powers!

This is **Shortcut volume 4, CONFIDENCE**. Welcome to the Alphas.

Dr. BAK NGUYEN

ANNEX

GLOSSARY OF Dr. BAK's LIBRARY

1

1SELF -080

REINVENT YOURSELF FROM ANY CRISIS
BY Dr. BAK NGUYEN

In 1SELF is about to reinvent yourself to rise from any crisis. Written in the midst of the COVID war, now more than ever, we need hope and the know-how to bridge the future. More than just the journey of Dr. Bak, this time, Dr. Bak is sharing his journey with mentors and people who built part of the world as we know it. Interviewed in this book, CHRISTIAN TRUDEAU, former CEO and FOUNDER of BCE EMERGIS (BELL CANADA), he also digitalized the Montreal Stock Exchange.RON KLEIN, American Innovator, inventor of the magnetic stripe of the credit card, of MLS (Multi-listing services) and the man who digitalized WALL STREET bonds markets.ANDRE CHATELAIN, former first vice-president of the MOVEMENT DESJARDINS. Dr. JEAN DE SERRES, former CEO of HEMA QUEBEC. These men created billions in values and have changed our lives, even without us knowing. They all come together to share their experiences and knowledge to empower each and everyone to emerge stronger from this crisis, from any crisis.

A

AFTERMATH -063
BUSINESS AFTER THE GREAT PAUSE
BY Dr. BAK NGUYEN & Dr. ERIC LACOSTE

In AFTERMATH, Dr. Bak joins forces with Community leader and philanthrope Dr. Eric Lacoste. Two powerful minds and forces of nature in the reaction to the worst economic meltdown in modern times. We are all victims

of the CORONA virus. Both just like humans have learned to adapt to survive, so is our economy. Most busines
structures and management philosophies are inherited from the age of industrialization and beyond. COVID-1
has shut down the world economy with months. At the time of the AFTERMATH, the truth is many corporation
and organizations will either have to upgrade to the INFORMATION AGE or disappear. More than th
INFORMATION upgrade, the era of SOCIAL MEDIA and the MILLENNIALS are driving a revolution in the cor
philosophy of all organizations. Profit is not king anymore, support is. In this time and age where a teenage
with a social account can compete with the million dollars PR firm, social implication is now the nev
cornerstone. Those who will adapt will prevail and prosper, while the resistance and old guards will soon b
forgotten as fossils of a past era.

ALPHA LADDERS -075
CAPTAIN OF YOUR DESTINY
BY Dr. BAK NGUYEN & JONAS DIOP

In ALPHA LADDERS, Dr. Bak is sharing his private conversation and board meetings with 2 of his trustee
lieutenants, strategist Jonas Diop and international Counsellor, Brenda Garcia. As both the Dr. Bak and ALPHA
brands are gaining in popularity and traction, it was time to get the movement to the next level. Now, it's abou
building a community and to help everyone willing to become ALPHAS to find their powers. Dr. Bak is a natura
recruiter of ALPHAS and peers. He also spent the last 20 years plus, training and mentoring proteges. Nov
comes the time to empower more and more proteges to become ALPHAS. ALPHAS LADDERS is the journey o
how Dr. Bak went from a product of Conformity to rise into a force of Nature, know as a kind tornado. In ALPHA
LADDERS Jonas pushed Dr. Bak to retrace each of the steps of his awakening, steps that we can breakdown anc
reproduce for ourselves. The goal is to empower each willing individual to become the ultimate Captain of his o
her destiny, and to do it, again and again. Welcome to the Alphas.

ALPHA LADDERS 2 -081
SHAPING LEADERS AND ACHIEVERS
BY Dr. BAK NGUYEN & BRENDA GARCIA

In ALPHA LADDERS 2, Dr. Bak is sharing the second part of his private conversation and board meetings with
his trusted lieutenants. This time it is with international Counsellor, Brenda Garcia that the dialogue is taking
place. In this second tome, the journey is taken to the next level. If the first tome was about the WHYs and the
HOWs at an individual level, this tome is about the WHYs and the HOWs at the societal level. Through the lens of
her background in international relations and diplomacy, Brenda now has the mission to help Dr. Bak establish
structures, not only for his emerging organization and legacy, THE ALPHAS, but to also inspire all the other
leaders and structures of our society. To do this, Brenda is taking Dr. Bak on an anthropological, sociological and
philosophical journey to revisit different historical key moments in various fields and eras, going as far back as
in ancient Greece at the dawn of democracy, all the way to the golden era of modern multilateralism embodied
by the UN structure. Learning from the legacies of prominent figures going from Plato to Ban Ki Moon, Martin
Luther King or Nelson Mandela, to Machiavelli, Marx and Simone de Beauvoir, Brenda and Dr. Bak are
attempting to grasp the essence of structure and hierarchy, their goal being to empower each willing individual
to become the ultimate Captain of their own success, to climb up the ladders no matter how high it is, and to
build their legacy one step at a time.

AMONGST THE ALPHAS -058
BY Dr. BAK NGUYEN, with Dr. MARIA KUNDSTATER, Dr. PAUL OUELLETTE and Dr. JEREMY KRELL

In AMONGST THE ALPHAS Dr. Bak opens the blueprint of the next level with the hope that everyone can be
better, bigger, wiser, but above all, a philosophy of Life that if, well applied, can bring inspiration to life. The
Alphas rose in the midst of the COVID war as an International Collaboration to empower individuals to rise from

the global crisis. Joining Dr. Bak are some of the world thinkers and achievers, the Alphas. Doctors, business people, thinkers, achievers, influencers, they are coming together to define what is an Alpha and his or her role, making the world a better place. This isn't the American dream, it is the human dream, one that can help you make History.Joining Dr. Bak are 3 Alpha authors, Dr. Maria Kundstater, Dr. Paul Ouellette and Dr. Jeremy Krell. This book started with questions from coach Jonas Diop. Welcome to the Alphas.

AMONGST THE ALPHAS vol.2 -059
ON THE OTHER SIDE
BY Dr. BAK NGUYEN with Dr. JULIO REYNAFARJE, Dr. LINA DUSEVICIUTE and Dr. DUC-MINH LAM-DO

In AMONGST THE ALPHAS 2, Dr. Bak continues to explore the meaning of what it is to be an Alpha and how to act amongst Alphas, because as the saying taught us: alone one goes fast, together we goes far. Some people see the problem. Some people look at the problem, some people created the problem. Some people leverage the problem into solutions and opportunities. Well, all of those people are Alphas. Networking and leveraging one another, their powers and reach are beyond measure. And one will keep the other in line too. Joining Dr. Bak are 3 Alphas from around the world coming together to share and collaborate, Dr. DUSEVICIUTE, Dr. LAM-DO and Dr. REYNAFARJE. This isn't the American dream, it is the human dream, one that can help you make History. Welcome to the Alphas.

B

BOOTCAMP -071
BOOKS TO REWRITE MINDSETS INTO WINNING STATES OF MIND
BY Dr. BAK NGUYEN

In BOOTCAMP 8 BOOKS TO REWRITE MINDSETS INTO WINNING STATES OF MIND, Dr. Bak is taking you into his past, before the visionary entrepreneur, before the world records, before the Industry's disruptor status. Here are 8 of the books that changed Dr. Bak's thinking and, therefore, reset his evolution into the course we now know him for. BOOTCAMP: 8 BOOKS TO REWRITE MINDSETS INTO WINNING STATES OF MIND, is a Bootcamp of 8 weeks for anyone looking to experience Dr. Bak's training to become THE Dr. BAK you came to know and love. This book will summarize how each title changed Dr. Bak mindset into a state of mind and how he applied that to rewrite his destiny. 8 books to read, that's 8 weeks of Bootcamp to access the power of your MIND and of your WILL. Are you ready for a change?

BRANDING -044
BALANCING STRATEGY AND EMOTIONS
BY Dr. BAK NGUYEN

BRANDING is communication to its most powerful state. Branding is not just about communicating anymore bu about making a promise, about establishing a relation, about generating an emotion. More than once, Dr. Ba proved himself to be a master, communicating and branding his ideas into flags attracting interest an influences, nationally and internationally. In BRANDING, Dr. Bak shares a very unique and personal journey branding Dr. Bak. How does he go from Dr. Nguyen, a loved and respected dentist to becoming Dr. Bak, a worl anchor hosting THE ALPHAS in the medical and financial world?More than a personal journey, BRANDING help to break down the steps to elevate someone with nothing else but the force of his or her spirit. Welcome to th Alphas.

C

CHANGING THE WORLD FROM A DENTAL CHAIR -007
BY Dr. BAK NGUYEN

Since he has received the EY's nomination for entrepreneur of the year for his startup Mdex & Co, Dr. Bak Nguyen has pushed the opportunity to the next level. Speaker, author, and businessman, Dr. Bak is a true entrepreneur and industries' disruptor. To compensate for the startup's status of Mdex & Co, he challenged himself to write a book based on the EY's questionnaire to share an in-depth vision of his company. With "Changing the World from a dental chair" Dr. Bak is sharing his thought process and philosophy to his approach to the industry. Not looking to revolutionize but rather to empower, he became, despite himself, an industries disruptor: an entrepreneur who has established a new benchmark. Dr. Bak Nguyen is a cosmetic dentist and visionary businessman who won the GRAND HOMAGE prize of "LYS de la Diversité" 2016, for his contribution as a citizen and entrepreneur in the community. He also holds recognitions from the Canadian Parliament and the Canadian Senate.

In 2003, he founded Mdex, a dental company upon which in 2018, he launched the most ambitious private endeavour to reform the dental industry, Canada wide. He wrote seven books covering ENTREPRENEURSHIP, LEADERSHIP, QUEST of IDENTITY, and now, PROFESSION HEALTH. Philosopher, he has close to his heart the quest of happiness of the people surrounding him, patients, and colleagues alike. Those projects have allowed Dr. Nguyen to attract interests from the international and diplomatic community and he is now the centre of a global discussion on the wellbeing and the future of the health profession. It is in that matter that he shares with you his thoughts and encourages the health community to share their own stories.

CHAMPION MINDSET -039
LEARNING TO WIN
BY Dr. BAK NGUYEN & CHRISTOPHE MULUMBA

CHAMPION MINDSET is the encounter of the business world and the professional sports world. Industries' Disruptor Dr. BAK NGUYEN shares his wisdom and views with the HAMMER, CFL Football Star, Edmonton's Eskimos CHRISTOPHE MULUMBA on how to leverage on the champion mindset to create successful entrepreneurs. Writing and challenging each other, they discovered the parallels and the difference of both worlds, but mainly, the recipe for leveraging from one to succeed in the other, from champions and entrepreneurs to WINNERS. Build and score your millions, it is a matter of mindset! This is CHAMPION MINDSET.

E

EMPOWERMENT -069
BY Dr. BAK NGUYEN

In EMPOWERMENT, Dr. Bak's 69th book, writing a book every 8 days for 8 weeks in a row to write the next world record of writing 72 books/36 months, Dr. Bak is taking a rest, sharing his inner feelings, inspiration, and motivation. Much more than his dairy, EMPOWERMENT is the key to walk in his footsteps and to comprehend the process of an overachiever. Dr. Bak's helped and inspired countless people to find their voice, to live their dream, and to be the better version of themselves. Why is he sharing as much and keep sharing? Why is he going that fast, always further and further, why and how is he keeping his inspiration and momentum? Those are all the answers EMPOWERMENT will deliver to you. This book might be one of the fastest Dr. Bak has written, not because of time constraints but from inspiration, pure inspiration to share and to grow. There is always a dark side to each power, two faces to a coin. Well, this is the less prominent facets of Dr. Bak Momentum and success, the road to his MINDSET.

F

FORCES OF NATURE -015
FORGING THE CHARACTER OF WINNERS
BY Dr. BAK NGUYEN

In FORCES OF NATURE, Dr. Bak is giving his all. This is his 15 books written within 15 months. It is the end of a marathon to set the next world record. For the occasion, he wanted to end with a big bang! How about a book with all of his biggest challenges? A Quest of Identity, a journey looking for his name and powers, Dr. Bak is borrowing with myths and legends to make this journey universal. Yes, this is Dr. Bak's mythology. Demons, heroes and Gods, there are forces of Nature that we all meet on our way for our name. Some will scare us, some will fight us, some will manipulate us. We can flee, we can hide, we can fight. What we do will define our next encounter and the one after. A tale of personal growth, a journey to find power and purpose, Dr. Bak is showing us the path to freedom, the Path of Life. Welcome to the Alphas.

H

HORIZON, BUILDING UP THE VISION -045
VOLUME ONE
BY Dr. BAK NGUYEN

Dr. Bak is opening up at your demand! Many of you are following Dr. Bak online and are asking to know more about his lifestyle. This is how he has chosen to respond: sharing his lifestyle as he traveled the world and what he learned in each city to come to build his Mindset as a driver and a winner. Here are 10 destinations (over 69 that will be following in the next volumes...) in which he shares his journey. New York, Quebec, Paris, Punta Cana, Monaco, Los Angeles, Nice, Holguin, the journey happened over twenty years.

HORIZON, ON THE FOOTSTEP OF TITANS -048
VOLUME TWO
BY Dr. BAK NGUYEN

Dr. Bak is opening up at your demand! Many of you are following Dr. Bak online and are asking to know more about his lifestyle. This is how he has chosen to respond: sharing his lifestyle as he traveled the world and what he learned in each city to come to build his Mindset as a driver and a winner. Here are 9 destinations (over 72 that will be following in the next volumes...) in which he shares his journey. Hong Kong, London, Rome, San Francisco, Anaheim, and more..., the journey happened over twenty years. Dr. Bak is sharing with you his feelings, impressions, and how they shaped his state of mind and character into Dr. Bak. From a dreamer to a driver and a builder, the journey started since he was 3. Wealth is a state of mind, and a state of mind is the basis of the drive. Find out about the mind of an Industry's disruptor.

HORIZON, Dr.EAMING OF THE FUTURE -068
VOLUME THREE
BY Dr. BAK NGUYEN

Dr. Bak is back. From the midst of confinement, he remembers and writes about what life was, when traveling was a natural part of Life. It will come back. Now more than ever, we need to open both our hearts and minds to fight fear and intolerance. Writing from a time of crisis, he is sharing the magic and psychological effect of seeing the world and how it has shaped his mindset. Here are 9 other destinations (over 75) in which he shares his journey. Beijing, Key West, Madrid, Amsterdam, Marrakech and more..., the journey happened over twenty years.

HOW TO NOT FAIL AS A DENTIST -047
BY Dr. BAK NGUYEN

In HOW TO NOT FAIL AS A DENTIST, Dr. Bak is given 20 plus years of experience and knowledge of what it is to be a dentist on the ground. PROFESSIONAL INTELLIGENCE, FINANCIAL INTELLIGENCE and MANAGEMENT INTELLIGENCE are the fields that any dentist will have to master for a chance to success and a shot for happiness practicing dentistry. Where ever you are starting your career as a new graduate or a veteran in the field looking to reach the next level, this is book smart and street smart all into one. This is Million Dollar Mindset applied to dentistry. We won't be making a millionaire out of you from this book, we will be giving you a shot to happiness and success. The million will follow soon enough.

HOW TO WRITE A BOOK IN 30 DAYS -042
BY Dr. BAK NGUYEN

In HOW TO WRITE YOUR BOOK IN 30 DAYS, Dr. Bak has crafted writing skills and techniques that can be shared and mastered. This book is mainly about structure and how to keep moving forward, avoiding the hit of the INSPIRATION WALL. You will find a wealth of wisdom from his experience writing your first, second, or even 10th book. Dr. Bak is sharing his secrets writing books, having written himself 72 books within 36 months. Visionary businessman, doctor in dentistry. Dr. Bak describes himself as a Dentist by circumstances, a communicator by passion, and an entrepreneur by nature.

HOW TO WRITE A SUCCESSFUL BUSINESS PLAN -049
BY Dr. BAK NGUYEN & ROUBA SAKR

In HOW TO WRITE A SUCCESSFUL BUSINESS PLAN, Dr. Bak is given 20 plus years of experience and knowledg of what it is to be an entrepreneur and more importantly, how to have the investors and banks on your side Being an entrepreneur is surely not something you learn from school, but there are steps to master so you ca communicate your views and vision. That's the only way you will have financing.Writing a business is only not mandatory stop only for the bankers, but an essential step to every entrepreneur, to know the direction an what's coming next. A business plan is also not set in stone, if there is a truth in business is that nothing will g as planned. Writing down your business plan the first time will prepare you to adapt and to overcome th challenges and surprises. For most entrepreneurs, a business is a passion. To most investors and all banks, . business is a system. Your business plan is the map to that system. However unique your ideas and busines are, the mapping follows the same steps and pattern.

HUMILITY FOR SUCCESS -051
BALANCING STRATEGY AND EMOTIONS
BY Dr. BAK NGUYEN

HUMILITY FOR SUCCESS is exploring the emotional discomforts and challenges champions, and overachievers put themselves through. Success is never done overnight and on the way, just like the pain and the struggle aren't enough, we are dealing with the doubts, the haters, and those who like to tell us how to live our lives anc what to do. At the same time, nothing of worth can be achieved alone. Every legend has a cast of characters allies, mentors, companions, rivals, and foes. So one needs the key to social behaviour. HUMILITY FOR SUCCESS is exploring the matter and will help you sort out beliefs from values, peers from friends. Humility is muct more about how we see ourselves than how others see us. For any entrepreneur and champion, our daily is tc set our mindset right, and to perfect our skills, not to fit in. There is a world where CONFIDENCE grows is ir synergy with HUMILITY. As you set the right label on the right belief, you will be able to grow and to leave the lies and haters far behinds. This is HUMILITY FOR SUCCESS.

HYBRID -011
THE MODERN QUEST OF IDENTITY
BY Dr. BAK NGUYEN

IDENTITY -004
THE ANTHOLOGY OF QUESTS
BY Dr. BAK NGUYEN

What if John Lennon was still alive and running for president today? What kind of campaign will he be running? IDENTIFY -THE ANTHOLOGY OF QUESTS is about the quest each of us has to undertake, sooner or later, THE QUEST OF IDENTITY. Citizen of the world, aim to be one, the one, one whole, one unity, made of many. That's the anthology of life! Start with your one, find your unity, and your legend will start. We are all small-minded people anyway! We need each other to be one! We need each other to be happy, so we, so you, so I, can be happy. This is the chorus of life. This is our song! Citizens of the world, I salute you! This is the first tome of the IDENTITY QUEST. FORCES OF NATURE (tome 2) will be following in SUMMER 2021. Also under development, Tome 3 - THE CONQUEROR WITHIN will start production soon.

INDUSTRIES DISRUPTORS -006
BY Dr. BAK NGUYEN

INDUSTRIES DISRUPTORS is a strange title, one that sparkles mixed feelings. A disruptor is someone making a difference, and since we, in general, do not like change, the label is mostly negative. But a disruptor is mostly someone who sees the same problem and challenge from another angle. The disruptor will tackle that angle and come up with something new from something existent. That's evolution! In INDUSTRIES DISRUPTORS, Dr. Bak is joining forces with James Stephan-Usypchuk to share with us what is going on in the minds and shoes of those entrepreneurs disrupting the old habits. Dr. Bak is changing the world from a dental chair, disrupting the dental, and now the book industry. James is a maverick in the Intelligence space, from marketing to Artificial Intelligence. Coming from very different backgrounds and industries, they end up telling very similar stories. If disruptors change the world, well, their story proves that disruptors can be made and forged. Here's the recipe. Here are their stories.

K

KRYPTO -040
TO SAVE THE WORLD
BY Dr. BAK NGUYEN & ILYAS BAKOUCH

L

LEADERSHIP -003
PANDORA'S BOX
BY Dr. BAK NGUYEN

LEADERSHIP, PANDORA'S BOX is 21 presidential speeches for a better tomorrow for all of us. It aims to drive HOPE and motivation into each and every one of us. Together we can make the difference, we hold such power Covering themes from LOYALTY to GENEROSITY, from FREEDOM and INTELLIGENCE to DOUBTS and DEATH, this is not the typical presidential or motivational speeches that we are used to. LEADERSHIP PANDORA'S BOX will surf your emotions first, only to dive with you to touch the core and soul of our meaning: to matter. This is not a Quest of Identity, but the cry to rally as a species, to raise our heads toward the future, and to move forward as a WHOLE. Not a typical Dr. Bak's book, LEADERSHIP, PANDORA'S BOX is a must-read for all of you looking for hope and purpose, all of us, citizens of the world.

LEVERAGE -014
COMMUNICATION INTO SUCCESS
BY Dr. BAK NGUYEN

In LEVERAGE COMMUNICATION TO SUCCESS, Dr. Bak shares his secret and mindsets to elevate an idea into a vision and a vision into an endeavour. Some endeavours will be a project, some others will become companies, and some will grow into a movement. It does not matter, each started with great communication.Communication is a very vast concept, education, sale, sharing, empowering, coaching, preaching, entertaining. Those are all different kinds of communication. The intent differs, the audiences vary, the messages are unique but the frame can be templated and mastered. In LEVERAGE COMMUNICATION TO SUCCESS, Dr. Bak is loyal to his core, sharing only what he knows best, what he has done himself. This book is dedicated to communicating successfully in business.

M

MASTERMIND, 7 WAYS INTO THE BIG LEAGUE -052
BY Dr. BAK NGUYEN & JONAS DIOP

MASTERMIND, 7 WAYS INTO THE BIG LEAGUE is the result of the encounter of business coach Jonas Diop and Dr. Bak. As a professional podcaster and someone always seeking the truth and ways to leverage success and performance, coach Jonas is putting Dr. Bak to the test, one that should reveal his secret to overachieve month after month, accumulating a new world record every month. Follow those two great minds as they push each other to surpass themselves, each in their own way and own style. MASTERMIND, 7 WAYS INTO THE BIG LEAGUE is more than a roadmap to success, it is a journey and a live testimony as you are turning the pages, one by one.

MIDAS TOUCH -065
POST-COVID DENTISTRY
BY Dr. BAK NGUYEN, Dr. JULIO REYNAFARJE AND Dr. PAUL OUELLETTE

MIDAS TOUCH, is the memoir of what happened in the ALPHAS SUMMIT in the midst of the GREAT PAUSE as great minds throughout the world in the dental field are coming together. As the time of competition is obsolete, the new era of collaboration is blooming. This is the 3rd book of the ALPHAS, after AFTERMATH and RELEVANCY, all written in the midst of confinement. Dr. Julio Reynafarje is bearing this initiative, to share with you the secret of a successful and lasting relationship with your patients, balancing science and psychology, kindness, and professionalism. He personally invited the ALPHAS to join as co-author, Dr. Paul Ouellette, and Dr.

Paul Dominique, and Dr. Bak.Together, they have more than 100 years of combined experience, wisdom, trade skills, philosophy, and secrets to share with you to empower you in the rebuilding of the dental profession in the aftermath of COVID. RELEVANCY was about coming together and to rebuild the future. MIDAS TOUCH is about how to build, one treatment plan at a time, one story at a time, one smile at a time.

MINDSET ARMORY -050
BY Dr. BAK NGUYEN

MINDSET ARMORY is Dr. Bak's 49th book, days after he completed his world record of writing 48 books within 24 months, on top of being a CEO of Mdex & Co and a full-time cosmetic dentist. Dr. Bak is undoubtedly an OVERACHIEVER. From his last books, he has shared more and more of his lifestyle and how it forged his winning mindset. Within MINDSET ARMORY, Dr. Bak is sharing with us his tools, how he found them, forged them, and leverage them. Just like any warrior needs a shield, a sword, and a ride, here are Dr. Bak's. For any entrepreneur, the road to success is a long and winding journey. On the way, some will find allies and foes. Some allies will become foes, and some foes might become allies. In today's competitive world, the only constant is change. With the right tool, it is possible to achieve. The right tool, the right mindset. This is MINDSET ARMORY.

MIRROR -085
BY Dr. BAK NGUYEN

MIRROR is the theme for a personal book. Not only to Dr. Bak but to all of us looking to reach beyond who and what we actually are. MIRROR is special in the fact that it is not only the content of the book that is of worth but the process in which Dr. Bak shared his own evolution. To go beyond who we are, one must grow every day. And how do you compare your growth and how far have you reach? Looking in the mirror. In all of Dr. Bak's writing, looking at the past is a trap to avoid at all costs. Looking in the mirror, is that any better? Share Dr. Bak's way to push and keep pushing himself without friction nor resistance. Please read that again. To evolve without friction or resistance... that is the source of infinite growth and the unification of the Quest for Power and the Quest of Happiness.

MOMENTUM TRANSFER -009
BY Dr. BAK NGUYEN & Coach DINO MASSON

How to be successful in your business and in your life? Achieve Your Biggest Goals With MOMENTUM TRANSFER. START THE BUSINESS YOU WANT - AND BRING IT NEXT LEVEL! GET THE LIFE YOU ALWAYS WANTED - AND IMPROVE IT! TAKE ANY PROJECTS YOU HAVE - AND MAKE IT THE BEST! In this powerful book, you'll discover what a small business owner learned from a millionaire and successful entrepreneur. He applied his mentor's principles and is explaining them in full detail in this book. The small business owner wrote the book he has always wanted to read and went from the verge of bankruptcy to quadrupling his revenues in less than 9 months and improve his personal life by increasing his energy and bring back peacefulness. Together, the millionaire and the small business owner are sharing their most valuable business and life lessons to the world. The most powerful book to increase your momentum in your business and your life introduces simple and radical life-changing concepts: Multiply your business revenues by finding the Eye of your Momentum - Increase your energy by building and feeding your own Momentum - How to increase your confidence with these simple steps - How to transfer your new powerful energy into other aspects of your business and life - How to set goals and achieve them (even crush them!)- How to always tap into an effortless and limitless force within you- And much, much more!

P

PLAYBOOK INTRODUCTION -055
BY Dr. BAK NGUYEN

In PLAYBOOK INTRODUCTION, Dr. Bak is open the door to all the newcomers and aspirant entrepreneurs who are looking at where and when to start. Based on questions of two college students wanting to know how to start their entrepreneurial journey, Dr. Bak dives into his experiences to empower the next generation, not about what they should do, but how he, Dr. Bak, would have done it today. This is an important aspect to recognize in the business world, the world has changed since the INFORMATION AGE and the advent of the millenniums into the market. Most matrix and know-how have to be adapted to today's speed and accessibility to the information. We are living at the INFORMATION AGE, this book is the precursor to the ABUNDANCE AGE, at least to those open to embrace the opportunity.

PLAYBOOK INTRODUCTION 2 -056
BY Dr. BAK NGUYEN

In PLAYBOOK INTRODUCTION 2, Dr. Bak continuing the journey to welcome the newcomers and aspirant entrepreneurs looking at where and when to start. If the first volume covers the mindset, the second is covering much more in-depth the concept of debt and leverage.This is an important aspect to recognize in the business world, the world has changed since the INFORMATION AGE and the advent of the millenniums into the market. Most matrix and know-how have to be adapted to today's speed and accessibility to the information. We are living at the INFORMATION AGE, this book is the precursor to the ABUNDANCE AGE, at least to those open to embrace the opportunity.

POWER -043
EMOTIONAL INTELLIGENCE
BY Dr. BAK NGUYEN

IN POWER, EMOTIONAL INTELLIGENCE, Dr. Bak is sharing his experiences and secrets leveraging on his EMOTIONAL INTELLIGENCE, a power we all have within. From SYMPATHY, having others opening up to you, to ACTIVE LISTENING, saving you time and energy; from EMPATHY, allowing you to predict the future to INFLUENCE, enabling you to draft the future, not to forget the power of the crowd with MOMENTUM, you are now in possession of power in tune with nature, yourself. It is a unique take on the subject to empower you to find your powers and your destiny. Visionary businessman, doctor in dentistry, Dr. Bak describes himself as a Dentist by circumstances, a communicator by passion, and an entrepreneur by nature.

POWERPLAY -078
HOW TO BUILD THE PERFECT TEAM

BY Dr. BAK NGUYEN

In POWERPLAY, HOW TO BUILD THE PERFECT TEAM, Dr. Bak is sharing with you his experience, perspectiv and mistake traveling the journey of the entrepreneur. A serial entrepreneur himself, he started venture on with a single partner as team to build companies with a director of human resources and a board of director POWERPLAY is not a story, it is the HOW TO build the perfect team, knowing that perfection is a lie. So how ca one build a team that will empower his or her vision? How to recruit, how to train, how to retain? Those are a legitimate questions. And all of those won't matter if the first question isn't answered: what is the reason fc the team? There is the old way to hire and the new way to recruit. Yes, Human Resources is all about mindse too! This journey is one of introspection, of leadership, and a cheat sheet to build, not only the perfect team bt the team that will empower your legacy to the next level.

PROFESSION HEALTH - TOME ONE -005
THE UNCONVENTIONAL QUEST OF HAPPINESS

BY Dr. BAK NGUYEN, Dr. MIRJANA SINDOLIC, Dr. ROBERT DURAND AND COLLABORATORS

Why are health professionals burning out while they give the best of themselves to heal the world? Dr. Bak aim to break the curse of isolation that health professionals face and establish a conversation to start the healin process. PROFESSION HEALTH is the basis of an ongoing discussion and will also serve as an introduction to study lead by Professor Robert Durand, DMD, MSc Science from University of Montreal, study co-financed b Mdex and the Federal Government of Canada. Co-writers are Dr. Mirjana Sindolic, Professor Robert Durand, Dr Jean De Serres, MD and former President of Hema Quebec, Counsel-Minister Luis Maria Kalaff Sanchez, Dr Miguel Angel Russo, MD, Banker Anthony Siggia, Banker Kyles Yves, and more...
This is the first Tome of three, dedicated to help "WHITE COATS" to heal and to find their happiness.

R

REBOOT -012
MIDLIFE CRISIS

BY Dr. BAK NGUYEN

MidLife Crisis is a common theme to each of us as we reach the threshold. As a man, as a woman, why is it that half of the marriages end up in recall? If anything else would have half those rates of failure, the lawsuits would be raining. Where are the flaws, the traps? Love is strong and pure, why is marriage not the reflection of that? All hard to ask questions with little or no answers. Dr. Bak is sharing his reflections and findings as he reached himself the WALL OF MARRIAGE. This is a matter that affects all of our lives. It is time for some answers.

RELEVANCY - TOME TWO -064
REINVENTING OURSELVES TO SURVIVE
BY Dr. BAK NGUYEN & Dr. PAUL OUELLETTE AND COLLABORATORS

THE GREAT PAUSE was a reboot of all the systems of society. Many outdated systems will not make it back. The Dental Industry is a needed one, it has laid on complacency for far too long. In an age where expertise is global and democratized and can be replaced with technologies and artificial intelligence, the REBOOT will force, not just an update, but an operating system replacement and a firmware upgrade.First, they saved their industry with THE ALPHAS INITIATIVE, sharing their knowledge and vision freely to all the world's dental industry. With the OUELLETTE INITIATIVE, they bought some time to all the dental clinics to resume and to adjust. The warning has been given, the clock is now ticking. who will prevail and prosper and who will be left behind, outdated and obsolete?

RISING -062
TO WIN MORE THAN YOU ARE AFRAID TO LOSE
BY Dr. BAK NGUYEN

In RISING, TO WIN MORE TAN YOU ARE AFRAID TO LOSE, Dr. Bak is breaking down the strategy to success to all, not only those wearing white coats and scrubs. More than his previous book (SUCCESS IS A CHOICE), this one is covering most of the aspects of getting to the next level, psychologically, socially, and financially. Rising is broken down into three key strategies: Financial Leverage - Compressing time ; Always being in control. Presented by MILLION DOLLAR MINDSET, the book is covering more than the ways to create wealth, but also how to reach happiness and to live a life without regrets. Dr. Bak the CEO and founder of Mdex & Co, a company with the promise of reforming the whole dental industry for the better. He wrote more than 60 books within 30 months as he is sharing his experiences, secrets, and wisdom.

S

SELFMADE -036
GRATITUDE AND HUMILITY
BY Dr. BAK NGUYEN

This is the story of Dr. Bak, an artist who became a dentist, a dentist who became an Entrepreneur, a Entrepreneur who is seeking to save an entire industry.In his free time, Dr. Bak managed to write 37 books an is a contender to 3 world records to be confirmed. Businessman and visionary, his views and philosophy ar ahead of our time. This is his 37th book. In SELFMADE, Dr. Bak is answering the questions most entrepreneur want to know, the HOWTO and the secret recipes, not just to succeed, but to keep going no matter wha SELFMADE is the perfect read for any entrepreneurs, novices, and veterans.

SUCCESS IS A CHOICE -060
BLUEPRINTS FOR HEALTH PROFESSIONALS
BY Dr. BAK NGUYEN

In SUCCESS IS A CHOICE, FINANCIAL MILLIONAIRE BLUEPRINTS FOR HEALTH PROFESSIONALS, Dr. Bak i breaking down the strategy to success for all those wearing white coats and scrubs: doctors, dentists pharmacists, chiropractors, nurses, etc. Success is broken down into three key strategies: Financial Leverage Compressing time - Always being in control. Presented by MILLION DOLLAR MINDSET, the book is coverin more than the ways to create wealth, but also how to reach happiness and to live a life without regrets.Dr. Ba is a successful cosmetic dentist with nearly 20 years of experience. He founded Mdex & Co, a company with th promise of reforming the whole dental industry for the better. While doing so, he discovered a passion fo writing and for sharing. Multiple times World Record, Dr. Bak is writing a book every 2 weeks for the last 3C months. This is his 60th book, and he is still practicing. How he does it, is what he is sharing with us, SUCCESS HAPPINESS, and mostly FREEDOM to all Health Professionals.

SYMPHONY OF SKILLS -001
BY Dr. BAK NGUYEN

You will enlighten the world with your potential. I can't wait to see all the differences that you will have in ou world. Remember that power comes with responsibility. We can feel in his presence, a genuine force, a depth o energy, confidence, innocence, courage, and intelligence. Bak is always looking for answers, morning and night he wants to understand the why and the why not. This book is the essence of the man. Dr. Bak is a force o nature who bears proudly his title eHappy. The man never ceases smiling nor spreading his good vibe whereve he passes. He is not trapped in the nostalgia of the past nor the satisfaction of the present, he embodies the joy of what's possible, what's to come. The more we read, the more we share, and we live. That is Bak, he charms us to evolve and to share his points of view, and before we know it, we are walking by his side, a journey we never saw coming.

T

THE 90 DAYS CHALLENGE -061
BY Dr. BAK NGUYEN

THE 90 DAYS CHALLENGE, is Dr. Bak's journey into the unknown. Overachiever writing 2 books a month on average, for the last 30 months, ambitious CEO, Industries' Disruptor, Dr. Bak seems to have success in everything he touches. Everything except the control of his weight. For nearly 20 years, he struggles with an overweight problem. Every time he scored big, he added on a little more weight. Well, this time, he exposes himself out there, in real-time and without filter, accepting the challenge of his brother-in-law, DON VO to lose 45 pounds within 90 days. That's half a pound a day, for three months. He will have to do so while keeping all of his other challenges on track, writing books at a world record pace, leading the dental industry into the new ERA, and keep seeing his patients. Undoubtedly entertaining, this is the journey of an ALPHA who simply won't give up. But this time, nothing is sure.

THE BOOK OF LEGENDS -024
BY Dr. BAK NGUYEN & WILLIAM BAK

The Book of Legends vol. 1 the story behind the world record of Dr. Bak and his son, William Bak. All Dr. Bak had in mind was to keep his promise of writing a book with his son. They ended up writing 8 children's books within a month, scoring a new world record. William is also the youngest author having published in two languages. Those are world records waiting to be confirmed. History will say: to celebrate a first world record (writing 15 books / 15 months), for the love of his son, he will have scored a second world record: to write 8 books within a month! THE BOOK OF LEGENDS vol. 1 This is both a magical journey for both a father and a son looking to connect and to find themselves. Join Dr. Bak and William Bak in their journey and their love for Life!

THE BOOK OF LEGENDS 2 -041
BY Dr. BAK NGUYEN & WILLIAM BAK

THE BOOK OF LEGENDS vol. 2 is the sequel of "CINDERELLA" but a true story between a father and his son. Together they have discovered a bond and a way to connect. The first BOOK OF LEGENDS covered the time of the first four books they wrote together within a month. The second BOOK OF LEGENDS is covering what happened after the curtains dropped, what happened after reality kicked back in. If the first volume was about a

225

fairy tale in vacation time, the second volume is about making it last in real Life. Share their journey and thei love of Life!

THE BOOK OF LEGENDS 3 -086
THE END OF THE INNOCENCE AGE
BY Dr. BAK NGUYEN & WILLIAM BAK

This is the third volume of the series, THE BOOK OF LEGENDS. If the first two happened as a breeze breaking world records on top of world records (27 books written as father and son), the 3rd volume took much more time to arrive. William has grown and writing chicken books is not enough anymore to ignite his imagination Dr. Bak, as a good father, will try to follow William's growth and invented new games, technics and mind frames to keep engaging William's imagination and interest. From auditions to backstories, Dr. Bak bent backward to keep the adventure going. More than sharing the success and the glory, within THE BOOK OF LEGENDS volume 3, you are sharing the doubts and failure of a father and son refusing to let go... but who have now left MOMENTUM... until the winds blow once more in their favour. Welcome to the Alphas.

THE CONFESSION OF A LAZY OVERACHIEVER -089
REINVENT YOURSELF FROM ANY CRISIS
BY Dr. BAK NGUYEN

In THE CONFESSION OF A LAZY OVERACHIEVER, Dr. Bak is opening up to his new marketing officer, Jamie, fresh out of school. She is young, full of energy, and looking to chill and still to have it all. True to his character, Dr. Bak is giving Jamie some leeway to redefine Dr. Bak's brand to her demographic, the Millennials. This journey is about Dr. Bak satisfying the Millennials and answering their true questions in life. A rebel himself, his ambition to change the world started back on campus, some 25 years ago... then, life caught up with him. It took Dr. Bak 20 years to shake down the burdens of life, to spread his wings free from Conformity, and to start Overachieving. Doctor, CEO, and world record author, here is what Dr. Bak would have love to know 25 years ago as was still on campus. In a word, this is cheating your way to success and freedom. And yes, it is possible. Success, Money, Freedom, it all starts with a mindset and the awareness of Time. Welcome to the Alphas.

THE ENERGY FORMULA -053
BY Dr. BAK NGUYEN

THE ENERGY FORMULA is a book dedicated to help each individual to find the means to reach their purpose and goal in Life. Dr. Bak is a philosopher, a strategist, a business, an artist, and a dentist, how does he do all of that? He is doing so while mentoring proteges and leading the modernization of an entire industry. Until now, Momentum and Speed were the powers that he was building on and from. But those powers come from somewhere too. From a guide of our Quest of Identity, he became an ally in everyone's journey for happiness. THE ENERGY FORMULA is the book revealing step by step, the logic of building the right mindset and the way to ABUNDANCE and HAPPINESS, universally. It is not just a HOW TO book, but one that will change your life and guide you to the path of ABUNDANCE.

THE MODERN WOMAN -070
TO HAVE IT HAVE WITH NO SACRIFICE
BY Dr. BAK NGUYEN & Dr. EMILY LETRAN

In THE MODERN WOMAN: TO HAVE IT ALL WITH NO SACRIFICE, Dr. Bak joins forces with Dr. Emily Letran to empower all women to fulfill their desires, goals, and ambition. Both overachievers going against the odds, they are sharing their experience and wisdom to help all women to find confidence and support to redefine their lives. Dr. Emily Letran is a doctor in dentistry, an entrepreneur, author, and CERTIFIED HIGH-PERFORMANCE coach. For an Asian woman, she made it through the norms and the red tapes to find her voice. As she learned and grew with mentors, today she is sharing her secret with the energy that will motivate all of the female genders to stand for what they deserve. Alpha doctor, Bak is joining his voice and perspective since this is not about gender equality, but about personal empowerment and the quest of Identity of each, man and woman. Once more, Dr. Bak is bringing LEVERAGE and REASON to the new social deal between man and woman. This is not about gender, but about confidence.

THE POWER BEHIND THE ALPHA -008
BY TRANIE VO & Dr. BAK NGUYEN

It's been said by a "great man" that "We are born alone and we die alone." Both men and women proudly repeat those words as wisdom since. I apologize in advance, but what a fat LIE! That's what I learned and discovered in life since my mind and heart got liberated from the burden of scars and the ladders of society. I can have it all, not all at the same time, but I can have everything I put my mind and heart into. Actually, it is not completely true. I can have most of what I and Tranie put our minds into. Together, when we feel like one, there isn't much out of our reach. If I'm the mind, she's the heart; if I'm the Will, she's the means. Synergy is the core of our power. Tranie's aim is always Happiness. In Tranie's definition of life, there are no justifications, no excuses, no tomorrow. For Tranie, Happiness is measured by the minutes of every single day. This is why she's so strong and can heal people around her. That may also be why she doesn't need to talk much, since talking about the past or the future is, in her mind, dimming down the magic of the present, the Now. We both respect and appreciate that we are the whole balancing each other's equation of life, of love, of success. I was the plus and the minus, then I became the multiplication factor and grew into the exponential. And how is Tranie evolving in all of this? She is and always will be the balance. If anything, she is the equal sign of each equation.

THE POWER OF Dr. -066
THE MODERN TITLE OF NOBILITY
BY Dr. BAK NGUYEN, Dr. PAVEL KRASTEV AND COLLABORATORS

In THE POWER OF Dr., independent thinkers mean to exchange ideas. An idea can be very powerful if supported with a great work ethic. Work ethic, isn't that the main fabric of our white coats, scrubs, and title? In an era post-COVID where everything has been rebooted and that the healthcare industry is facing its own fate: to evolve or to be replaced, Dr. Bak and Dr. Pavel reveal the source of their power and their playbook to move forward, ahead. The power we all hold is our resilience and discipline. We put that for years at the service of our profession, from a surgical perspective. Now, we can harness that same power to rewrite the rules, the industry, and our future. Post-COVID, the rules are being rewritten, will you be part of the team or left behind?
"You can be in control!" More than personal growth and a motivational book, THE POWER OF Dr. is an awakening call to the doctor you look at when you graduate, with hope, with honour, with determination.

THE POWER OF YES -010
VOLUME ONE: IMPACT
BY Dr. BAK NGUYEN

In THE POWER OF YES, Dr. Bak is sharing his journey opening up and embracing the world, one day at a time, one ask at a time, one wish at a time. Far from a dare, saying YES allowed Dr. Bak to rewrite his mindsets and to break all the boundaries. This book is not one written a few days or weeks, but the accumulation of a journey for 12 months. The journeys started as Dr. Bak said YES to his producer to go on stage and to speak... That YES opened a world of possibilities. Dr. Bak embraced each and every one of them. 12 months later, he is celebrating the new world record of writing 9 books written over a period of 12 months. To him, it will be a miss, missing the 12 on 12 mark. To the rest of the world, they just saw the birth of a force of nature, the Alpha force. THE POWER OF YES is comprised of all the introduction of the adult books written by Dr. Bak within th first 12 months. Chapter by chapter, you can walk in his footstep seeing and smelling what he has. This reality literature with a twist of POWER. THE POWER OF YES! Discover your potential and your power. This the POWER OF YES, volume one. Welcome to the Alphas.

THE POWER OF YES 2 -037
VOLUME TWO: SHAPELESS
BY Dr. BAK NGUYEN

In THE POWER OF YES, volume 2, Dr. Bak is continuing his journey discovering his powers and influence. Afte 12 months embracing the world saying YES, he rose as an emerging force: he's been recognized as a INDUSTRIES DISRUPTOR, got nominated ERNST AND YOUNG ENTREPRENEUR OF THE YEAR, wrote 9 book within 12 months while launching the most ambitious private endeavour to reform his own industry, the denta field. Contender too many WORLD RECORDS, Dr. Bak is doing all of that in parallel. And yes, he is sleeping hi nights and yes, he is writing his book himself, from the screen of his iPhone! Far from satisfied, Dr. Bak misse the mark of writing 12 books within 12 months and everything else is shaping and moving, and could com crumbling down at each turn. Now that Dr. Bak understands his powers, he is looking to test them and to pus them to their limits, looking to keep scoring world records while materializing his vision and enterprises. Thi is the awakening of a Force of Nature looking to change the world for the better while having fu sharing. Welcome to the Alphas.

THE POWER OF YES 3 -046
VOLUME THREE: LIMITLESS
BY Dr. BAK NGUYEN

In THE POWER OF YES, volume 3, the journey of Dr. Bak continues where the last volume left, in front of 30 plus people showing up to his first solo event, a Dr. Bak's event. On stage and in this book, Dr. Bak reveals how 12 months saying YES to everything changed his life... actually, it was 18 months.
From a dentist looking to change the world from a dental chair into a multiple times world record author, th journey of openness is a rendez-vous with Fate. Dr. Bak is sharing almost in real-time his journey, experiences but above all, his feelings, doubts, and comebacks. From one book to the next, from one journey to the next follow the adventure of a man looking to find his name, his worth, and his place in the world. Doing so, he i touching people Doing so, he is touching people and initiating their rises. Are you ready for more? Are you ready to meet your Fate and Destiny? Welcome to the Alphas.

THE POWER OF YES 4 -087
VOLUME FOUR: PURPOSE
BY Dr. BAK NGUYEN

In THE POWER OF YES, volume 4, the journey continues days after where the last volume left. After setting the new world record of writing 48 books within 24 months, Dr. Bak is not ready to stop. As volume one covers 12 months of journey, volume 2 covers 6 months. Well, volume 3 covers 4 months. The speed is building up and increasing, steadily. This is volume 4, RISING, after breaking the sound barrier. Dr. Bak has reached a state where he is above most resistance and friction, he is now in a universe of his own, discovering his powers as he walks his journeys. This is no fiction story or wishful thinking, THE POWER OF YES is the journey of Dr. Bak, from one world record to the next, from one book to the next. You too can walk your own legend, you just need to listen to your innersole and to open up to the opportunity. May you get inspiration from the legendary journey of Dr. Bak and find your own Destiny. Welcome to the Alphas.

THE RISE OF THE UNICORN -038
BY Dr. BAK NGUYEN & Dr. JEAN DE SERRES

In THE RISE OF THE UNICORN, Dr. Bak is joining forces with his friend and mentor, Dr. Jean De Serres. Together both men had many achievements in their respective industries, but the advent of eHappyPedia, THE RISE OF THE UNICORN is a personal project dear to both of them: the QUEST OF HAPPINESS and its empowerment. This book is a special one since you are witnessing the conversation between two entrepreneurs looking to change the world by building unique tools and media. Just like any enterprise, the ride is never a smooth one in the park on a beautiful day. But this is about eHappyPedia, it is about happiness, right? So it will happen and with a smile attached to it! The unique value of this book is that you are sharing the ups and downs of the launch of a Unicorn, not just the glory of the fame, but also the doubts and challenges on the way. May it inspire you on your own journey to success and happiness.

THE RISE OF THE UNICORN 2 -076
eHappyPedia
BY Dr. BAK NGUYEN & Dr. JEAN DE SERRES

This is 2 years after starting the first tome. Dr. Bak's brand is picking up, between the accumulation of records and the recognition. eHappyPedia is now hot for a comeback. In THE RISE OF THE UNICORN 2, Dr. Bak is retracing and addressing each of Dr. Jean De Serres' concerns about the weakness of the first version of eHappyPedia and the eHappy movement. This is the sort of the creation and a UNICORN both in finance and in psychology. Never before, you will assist in such daily and decision-making process of a world phenomenon and of a company. Dr. Bak and Dr. De Serres are literally using the process of writing this series of books to plan and to brainstorm the birth of a bluechip. More than an intriguing story, this is the journey of 2 experienced entrepreneurs changing the world.

THE U.A.X STORY -072
THE ULTIMATE AUDIO EXPERIENCE
BY Dr. BAK NGUYEN

This is the story of the ULTIMATE AUDIO EXPERIENCE, U.A.X. Follow Dr. Bak's footstep on how he invented a new way to read and to learn. Dr. Bak brings his experience as a movie producer and a director to elevate the reading experience to another level with entertaining value and make it accessible to everyone, auditive, and visual people alike.

Three years plus of research and development, countless hours of trials and errors, Dr. Bak finally solved his puzzle: having written more than 1.1 million words. The irony is that he does not like to read, he likes audiobooks! U.A.X. finally allowed the opening of Dr. Bak's entire library to a new genre and media. U.A.X. is the new way to learn and enjoy Audiobooks. Made to be entertaining while keeping the self-educational value of a book, U.A.X. will appeal to both auditive and visual people. U.A.X. is the blockbuster of the Audiobooks. The format has already been approved by iTunes, Amazon, Spotify, and all major platforms for global distribution and streaming.

THE VACCINE -077
BY Dr. BAK NGUYEN & WILLIAM BAK

In THE VACCINE, A TALE OF SPIES AND ALIENS, Dr. Bak reprise his role as mentor to William, his 10 years-old son, both as co-author and as doctor. William is living through the COVID war and has accumulated many, many questions. That morning, they got out all at once. From a conversation between father and son, Dr. Bak making science into words keeping the interest of his son a Saturday morning in bed. William is not just an audience, he is responsible to map the field with his questions. What started as a morning conversation between father and son, became within the next hour, a great project, their 23rd book together. Learn about the virus, vaccination while entertaining your kids.

TO OVERACHIEVE EVERYTHING BEING LAZY -090
CHEAT YOUR WAY TO SUCCESS
BY Dr. BAK NGUYEN

In TO OVERACHIEVE EVERYTHING BEING LAZY, Dr. Bak retaking his role talking to the millennials, the new generation. If in the first tome of the series LAZY, Dr. Bak addresses the general audience of millennials, especially young women, he is dedicating this tome to the ALPHA amongst the millennials, those aiming for the moon and looking, not only to be happy but to change the world. This is not another take on how to cheat your way to success or how to leverage laziness, but this is the recipe to build overachievers and rainmakers. For the young leaders with ambitions and talent, understanding TIME and ENERGY are crucial from your first step writing your our legend. If Dr. Bak had the chance to do it all over again, this is how he would do it! Welcome the Alphas.

TORNADO -067
FORCE OF CHANGE
BY Dr. BAK NGUYEN

In TORNADO - FORCE OF CHANGE Dr. Bak is writing solo. In the midst of the COVID war, change is not a good intention anymore. Change, constant change has become a new reality, a new norm. From somebody who hold the title of Industries' Disruptor, how does he yield change to stay in control? Well, the changes from the COVID war are constant fear and much loss of individual liberty. Some can endure the change, some will ride it. Dr. Bak is sharing his angle of navigating the changes, yielding the improvisations, and to reinvent the goals, the means to stay relevant. From fighting to keep his companies Dr. Bak went on to let go the uncontrollable to embrace the opportunity, he reinvented himself to ride the change and create opportunities from an unprecedented crisis. This is the story of a man refusing to kneel and accept defeat, smiling back at faith to find leverage and hope.

TOUCHSTONE -073
LEVERAGING TODAY'S PSYCHOLOGICAL SMOG
BY Dr. BAK NGUYEN & Dr. KEN SEROTA

TOUCHSTONE, LEVERAGING TODAY'S PSYCHOLOGICAL SMOG is mapping to navigate and to thrive in today's high and constant stress environment. After 40 years in practice, Dr. Serota is concerned about the evolution of the career of health care professionals and the never-ending level of stress. What is stress, what are its effects, damages, and symptoms? If COVID-19 revealed to the world that we are fragile, it also revealed most of the broken and the flaws of our system. For now a century, dentistry has been a champion in depression, Dr.ug addiction, and suicide rate, and the curve is far from flattening. Dr. Bak is sharing his perspective and experience dealing with stress and how to leverage it into a constructive force. From the stress of a doctor with no right to failure to the stress of an entrepreneur never knowing the future, Dr. Bak is sharing his way to use stress as leverage.

ABOUT THE AUTHORS

From Canada, **Dr BAK NGUYEN**, Nominee Ernst and Young Entrepreneur of the year, Grand Homage Lys DIVERSITY, and LinkedIn & TownHall Achiever of the year. Dr Bak is a cosmetic dentist, CEO and founder of Mdex & Co. His company is revolutionizing the dental field. Speaker and motivator, he wrote 72 books over 36 months accumulating many world records (to be officialized).

- **ENTREPRENEURSHIP**
- **LEADERSHIP**
- **QUEST OF IDENTITY**
- **DENTISTRY AND MEDICINE**
- **PARENTING**
- **CHILDREN BOOKS**
- **PHILOSOPHY**

In 2003, he founded Mdex, a dental company upon which in 2018, he launched the most ambitious private endeavour to reform the dental industry, Canada wide. Philosopher, he has close to his heart the quest of happiness of the people surrounding him, patients and colleagues alike. In 2020, he launched an International collaborative initiative named **THE ALPHAS** to share knowledge and for Entrepreneurs and Doctors to thrive through the Greatest Pandemic and Economic depression of our time.

In 2016, he co-found with Tranie Vo, Emotive World Incorporated, a tech research company to use technology to empower happiness and sharing. U.A.X. the ultimate audio experience is the landmark project on which the team is advancing, utilizing the technics of the movie industry and the advancement in ARTIFICIAL INTELLIGENCE to save the book industry and to upgrade the continuing education space.

These projects have allowed Dr Nguyen to attract interests from the international and diplomatic community and he is now the center of a global discussion in the wellbeing and the future of the health profession. It is in that matter that he shares his thoughts and encourages the health community to share their own stories.

"It's not worth it go through it alone! Together, we stand, alone, we fall."

Motivational speaker and serial entrepreneur, philosopher and author, from his own words, Dr Nguyen describes himself as a dentist by circumstances, an entrepreneur by nature and a communicator by passion.

He also holds recognitions from the Canadian Parliament and the Canadian Senate.

www.DrBakNguyen.com

UAX

ULTIMATE AUDIO EXPERIENCE

A new way to learn and enjoy Audiobooks. Made to be entertaining while keeping the self-educational value of a book, UAX will appeal to both auditive and visual people. UAX is the blockbuster of the Audiobooks.

UAX will cover most of Dr Bak's books, and is now negotiating to bring more authors and more titles to the UAX concept. Now streaming on Spotify, Apple Music and available for download on all major music platforms. Give it a try today!

FROM THE SAME AUTHOR
Dr Bak Nguyen

www.DrBakNguyen.com

CHILDREN'S BOOK
with William Bak

The Trilogy of Legends

THE SPIES AND ALIENS COLLECTION

SHORTCUT

SOCIETY

www.DrBakNguyen.com

AMAZON - BARNES & NOBLE - APPLE BOOKS - KINDLE
SPOTIFY - APPLE MUSIC

DR.
Bak Nguyen